A. Anonymous

Don't Forget to Tape the Toilets: *The Missing Employee Orientation Manual for Saudi Arabia and Bahrain*

©2012, 2014 Andalus Publishing

This low-priced e-book has been completely set in a type face designed for easy reading and was printed from new plates. It contains the complete text of the original hard-cover edition. Not one word has been omitted.

Don't Forget to Tape the Toilets: The Missing Employee Orientation Manual for Saudi Arabia and Bahrain

ISBN: 978-0-9910476-2-8

This book may not be reproduced in whole or in part, by mimeograph or any other means, without permission. For information address: admin@alanduspublishing.com

Contents

Saudi Arabia	3
Before Leaving	4
Visas	7
Arrival	14
Hotel	22
One Office to Rule them All	24
Work Week	27
Driving	30
Crossing the Border	35
Housing	42
Electricity	48
Water	51

CONTENTS

Mail	**60**
Communications	**62**
Khobar Attacks	**65**
Reading List	**67**
Bahrain	**70**
Language	**74**
Police	**79**
Gender	**83**
Diversity	**89**
Alcohol	**91**
Religion	**96**
Ramadan	**101**
Supernatural	**105**
Navy Base	**109**
Weekend Travel	**112**
Slavery	**116**
Lies	**118**

Banking	**120**
Saudiization	**126**
Miscellaneous	**128**
The Work	**135**
Basic Information	**136**

CONTENTS

Introduction

The purpose of this guide is to provide a completely biased and idiosyncratic review of information that I have accumulated during my time in Saudi Arabia and which I hope will be useful for the prospective visitor or the newly arrived employee to the Kingdom.

The eyes of the traveler, seeing dissonances, are useful even for the local inhabitants whose senses can be dulled by the repetition of daily life. I hope that I have not lived in the Kingdom so long as to have forgotten everything that was unusual or which required coping or attitude adjustments. There are things the local residents take for granted that the visitor will find outrageous. Still, over the past decade I have been in and out of the Kingdom often enough, I hope, to have kept my traveler's eyes.

In 2010 Yorks tried to compile an employee manual for the Gulf but because of unsettled political issues–and by this I do not mean unrest amongst the Khalifa or the Al-Saud–kicked the can down the road where it still rests today. An institution like Yorks would normally be expected to give orientation advice to employees and new arrivals. Part of the problem is that the term "employee" here in the Gulf is a bit problematic: we have all sorts of *sui generis* creatures who do not fit into the Yorks zoology. Some are Yorks partners, some are employed by Yorks-controlled entities, some are employed by Yorks Services, Inc. and others are employed by a local firm with whom Yorks has an exclusive relationship. That means that the individuals working together will be covered by different employment regimes altogether. Since the term "employee" cannot be defined generally it is not clear in what sense this can really be an employee manual. When a project starts with a disputed definition it is unlikely that it can be completed to everyone's satisfaction. Recognizing therefore that the Yorks employee manual for the Gulf will never be finished, this text is offered as a way to bridge the gap between what should be and what is.

Last year a prospective hire from Calgary visited Saudi Arabia. He was considering working in the Gulf offices for a time and wanted to get the lay of the land. Because there is no employee manual, when I met with him I handed him a legal pad and told him to take notes. In a way, this text grew out of those conversations. It is difficult to condense what you should know in just a few pages. There is a lot to know in order to make an informed decision about accepting a new position or transfer to the Gulf. Perhaps this effort will be more useful since it pretends to be more comprehensive. Later, it occurred to me that others might benefit from this information even if they have no relationship to Yorks.

Skimming through the Table of Contents you may say to yourself, "I know this stuff." Trust me. You don't.

All of the information herein is utterly and completely biased and the personal opinion of the author. Furthermore, not only is the information biased, but in many cases is based on double or triple hearsay–though you should know that in Islamic law this is not necessarily a bad thing. Other information is unverifiable, and like Saudi Arabia itself, contradictory.

All of the above is to say that I take no responsibility for what follows. Use at your own risk.

Saudi Arabia

Saudi Arabia is one of the most visited countries on the planet and at the same time one of the most difficult countries to visit. Saudi Arabia is roughly the size of the United States east of the Mississippi River. It is a four hour and four hundred kilometer drive from Riyadh to Khobar, and a 1000 kilometer drive from Riyadh to Jeddah.

The basic truth about Saudi Arabia is that any statement about the country is both equally true and false. If you make a statement about Saudi Arabia which someone contradicts both of you are right. This is difficult for most people to understand.

Before Leaving

Shipping Personal Effects

It is important to plan well prior to leaving for Saudi Arabia. If you are coming for a one to to two year assignment, Yorks will reimburse you for shipping your household goods. You had best use a company that has experience in this area. It makes more sense to use a company in Bahrain; a North American company will happily come to your home to pack and ship your household goods, but after dispatch will be of little help. You will need someone local at the receiving end with whom you have a contractual relationship in case something goes wrong.

If you are coming for a short period of time, you are on your own. Pay no attention to anyone who says you should ship household goods, personal effects or even mail directly to Al Khobar.

You are usually better off sending packages to Bahrain than to Saudi. Bahrain is a mail and courier hub while the Eastern Province is, well, Saudi Arabia. Goods sent to the Eastern Province are trucked over from Bahrain at additional cost with delivery delayed. Because of Saudi customs eccentricities and delays, it makes more sense to send mail, including small packages, to the Bahrain office.

There will be many household items that you wish to take with you when you come to the Gulf. Try to resist the temptation. A common sight at the airport is a traveler paying excess baggage charges for six or seven bags. There are few items that you will not be able to replace when you arrive. Moreover, they will be adapted to local conditions and more likely than not, will do the job expected of them. If you cannot live without that George Foreman grill do not worry, you can buy one locally. If you must bring items, consider shipping them to the office in advance. The firm's Bahrain address is:

Yorks
Big Office Building
P.O. Box 1234567890
Manama, Bahrain
Tel.: +973 12 34 56 78

Bahrain does not use postal codes of any kind. Many computerized systems (including Amazon.com) will insist on the input of a postal code to validate an address. If this is required, use four ("0000") or five zeroes: "00000".

Accompanied baggage is not subject to customs duties in Saudi Arabia. You may find it convenient to ship books and heavier items, especially if you plan to make a stopover on your way to your new home.

International Driver's License

Before leaving, obtain an international driver's license. These are issued for a nominal fee by the Canadian Automobile Association or the American Automobile Association. Two passport size photographs are required. Otherwise you will have to obtain either a Saudi or Bahraini license. While some companies (such as Saudi Aramco) provide assistance so that their employees can obtain local operator's licenses, Yorks has no such facilities and provides no assistance. You are on your own.

Photographs

Bring about twenty passport-size photographs of yourself before you come. You will need them for all sorts of different reasons, including obtaining local identification cards such as the access cards for the Remote Saudi Office Building and the Big Office Building in Bahrain. If you decide to join the British Club in Bahrain you will need two photographs as well. You can join even though you live and work in Al Khobar and do not possess British nationality. There are benefits to membership, especially during Ramadan.

Visas

Visas

A visitor cannot simply travel to Saudi Arabia upon a whim. An invitation must first be sent and a visa issued for a visitor before permission is granted to enter the country. There are currently two ways to get a visa invitation letter in addition to a supplemental procedure for Yorks in the Gulf. The first way is to contact the Saudi Arabia General Investment Authority (SAGIA) (http://sagia.gov.sa) and tell them that you are interested in making an investment in Saudi Arabia. If you have a business of your own (or work for a company like Yorks) they will send you a visa invitation letter. Make sure the invitation letter requests that you be given a multiple entry/exit visa.

Getting the visa requires filling out an application, supplying two photographs, paying a fee in the range of $100 and having a passport with at least six months validity remaining on it with at least two blank facing pages. You enter your details into the on-line *Enjaz* system in order to obtain a visa block number. Assemble the documents, put the package together and forward it to the closest Saudi Embassy or consulate and normally within a few days your passport will be returned to you with your visa.

A prepaid courier envelope (or US Express mail or its equivalent) should accompany the application so that the passport can be tracked both ways. Customarily, a Saudi company will issue business visit visa invitation letters to those that it seeks to do business with and the procedure is routine. Yorks in the Gulf has a supplemental procedure involving the Saudi Embassy in London. Other companies may not be so privileged.

There is a Saudi Embassy in Washington and Ottawa. Both have consular sections. There is a Saudi consulate in New York and Houston, but you must live in either consular district in order to be able to submit your application there.

In the past, visas were usually issued for either three or six months. Unfortunately, the calculation was based on Hejira months which have only 28 days. The visa's term starts upon issuance, not upon arrival in the Kingdom. Because getting in and out of Saudi Arabia can be difficult away from the Eastern Province, it is all too easy to make a mistake and overstay the visa. The penalty for overstaying a visa is SR 10,000 and will not be waived. Now visas state the number of days they are valid so it is easier to see when they expire. However, the penalty remains the same.

Make sure to get your application in early. Tit for tat diplomatic retaliation means Canadians have to wait twenty-two days before their passports are processed. This means that a Canadian passport will sit on someone's desk at the consular section in Ottawa for nearly a month before an official even looks at it.

If you are going to work in Saudi Arabia you need a residency visa or work permit. *Iqama* is the Arabic name given to the Saudi residency permit. There are two kinds of ***Iqama***: one allows the holder the right to work, the other is held by the worker's dependents. The *iqama* usually is valid for a year, but may be issued for two years. After its expiration, the *iqama* can be renewed. If you are asked to obtain a local *iqama* your sponsor will be your Saudi employer. The *iqama* process starts with a visa invitation letter and a similar process like that involved for the business visit visa. There are two extra steps which require that you undergo a medical examination and have your professional degrees certified. The latter can take a good deal of time, depending on how responsive your university is. The degrees have to be notarized, the notary's authority certified and that certification must receive an apostille at the national level after which the documentation is forwarded to the Saudi Embassy.

Upon arriving in Saudi Arabia the medical exam must be repeated and your passport turned into the *Jahwazat*, or passport office. They will hold your passport for approximately one to two weeks while your *iqama* is prepared. Current *iqamas* look like credit cards and bear your picture. Older *iqamas* look like passports and have a green cover. During the time your *iqama* is being prepared you cannot leave the country for any reason. During this *iqama* processing time the word "emergency" does not exist for you, so please try to arrange your affairs to that you do not have an emergency requiring you to leave the country while your passport is at the passport office.

Once your *iqama* is issued, your Saudi employer has the right to keep you from returning to Saudi Arabia to work for another employer for a two year period after your final exit. This is so even though there is no provision for such a requirement in the Saudi Labor Law. There is such a provision in the Saudi Labor Law Implementing Regulations, but it is hard to see what provision of the Labor Law this rule purports to implement. Prior to obtaining an *iqama*, you should obtain your employer's consent in advance to transfer your *iqama* to another employer or to issue a no-objection letter at the time your employment contract is signed. Otherwise you may never get the no objection letter at all. This advice is somewhat impractical, for nothing will sour contract negotiations like the mention of the possibility of your employment with a competitor. One discreet way around the issue is to ask for a transferable *iqama*.

You should make sure that your *iqama* permits multiple exits and entries, otherwise you will be in the country until the expiration of the *iqama*.

In order to leave the country upon the expiration of the *iqama* or upon termination of employment an exit-only or final exit permission is required. Without this, you will not be permitted to cross the border or get on an airplane. Obtaining the final exit takes about a week.

About the *Iqama* (Residence Permit)

Is there an advantage to having an *iqama*?
Not really.

Having an *iqama* permits you to open a bank account, invest in the Saudi stock market ("Tadawul") or purchase an automobile in your own name. However, if your employment terminates or if you *iqama* expires–or if a mistake has made and somehow you are placed on a list of the no-longer employed or if your *iqama* is listed as having expired though it is still valid–your bank account will be frozen and it will be impossible to access your funds. There have been cases that have required the intervention of a country's ambassador to solve this problem and in the meantime the former *iqama* holder was reduced to penury.

This is a problem that Saudi Arabia has been unable to solve and which happens all too often. If you have a business visit visa, you will not see any difference on a day to day basis merely because you do not have an *iqama*. On balance, having a Saudi bank account is not worth the trouble.

If your duty assignment is Bahrain, Yorks will obtain for you the Bahraini equivalent of the *iqama*, which is called a CPR (Certificate of Personal Residence). While a visa is required to visit Bahrain, visas can be obtained at the airport for most Western nationalities, though the onset of civil unrest in the country has caused a temporary suspension of local visa issuance for some nationalities and a requirement that visas be obtained at Bahraini embassies. Visas otherwise are normally issued at the airport for a thirty-day period which can be renewed in-country before the expiration of the visa without too much difficulty. It is better to state your occupation as "consultant" because of possible local restrictions on other professions. Students, political activists and journalists are subject to heightened scrutiny.

The penalty for overstaying a Bahraini visa is BD 40, or about $100 USD. In comparison, the penalty for overstaying a Saudi visa is much greater: SAR 10,000 ($2667 USD) and the penalty will not be waived.

If your duty station is Saudi Arabia, as far as Yorks is concerned, in Bahrain you are on your own. Expect no help when it comes to regularizing your status in Bahrain. Each time you cross over into Bahrain on your Saudi visa you will pay a SR 50 fee. If you get tired of the fee, for BD 100 or so you can obtain a visa valid for five years which permits you stays up to thirty days at a time. If you do not have a Saudi visa, a visa run can be made to Qatar or to Dubai. If you are working in the Bahrain office and need a Saudi visa this will be obtained for you. Funny how Yorks fails to extend such courtesies to those on the other side of the border.

If you have a CPR you can obtain a Saudi visa in Bahrain, otherwise you will have to send your passport to Canada, London or the United States. If you need to leave the country during this time you will be inconvenienced unless you obtain a second passport. You can do so in both the United States and Canada by explaining to the relevant authorities your need to have a travel document while your passport is touring various embassies waiting to be filled with visas. Usually the second passport is for a limited duration (in the case of the United States, one year), but it will still get you out of the country (well, at least Bahrain) in an emergency. Remember, you are not permitted to have emergencies in Saudi Arabia.

Many will tell you that without a Bahraini CPR you cannot get a mobile phone, Internet, rent a car or the like. This is not true. Without a CPR you cannot open a bank account; however, you should be able to accomplish all of the rest with your passport. It may even be that it is possible to open a bank account due to the new Bahrain/U.S. Free Trade Agreement and the presence of U.S. Military personnel (almost none of whom have CPR's) in the country. Since these rules can change at any time, all you can do is ask.

The Matter of Sponsorship

One issue that is often the subject of friction is that of sponsorship in the Kingdom. This topic only applies to Yorks employees based in Al Khobar; if this is not you, read on. For this discussion, we will also have to assume that you are not receiving money from Canada. Since everyone receives money from Canada this discussion is somewhat hypothetical, but in the Kingdom of Magic we do not let reality or contradiction stand in our way.

The Kingdom realizes that the sponsorship system is archaic and functions as a drag on business. Proposals have been floated to abolish the system, but whether these are sincere or merely an effort to forestall criticism is unknown. In any event, given the glacial speed of change in Saudi Arabia, do not expect the announced changes to take effect any time soon.

Yorks employees based in Bahrain do not have to put up with this nonsense. Yorks will secure a Saudi business visit visa for those times when it is necessary or desirable to meet with clients in the Kingdom. When your Saudi business visit visa expires another will be obtained for you without a whimper. There is no restriction on the number of business visit visas you can have. Pay no attention to anyone who tells you otherwise.

Arrival

Travel to the Gulf

A traditional Arab proverb commands "guard thy travels and thy treasure. This advice made good sense in the days of the caravans as these were subject to attack by Bedouin raiders. The likelihood of Bedouins mounting a raid on one of Saudia Airlines night flights from Jeddah or Riyadh seems unlikely, but you can never be completely sure. The custom of lying about one's whereabouts has never changed but when translated to the context of the modern consulting office, hilarity can ensue.

There are many different routes to Saudi Arabia from North America. Saudia, the Saudi national airline, flies from New York and Washington to Jeddah and then on to Riyadh without switching equipment. In the summer, there are even flights from the Disney paradise Orlando. No alcohol is served on board and the entertainment options are, shall we say, somewhat limited.

Compared to Saudia, on Gulf Air, to paraphrase a poet, "life is a festival...where all wines flow." Though there are Bahraini restrictions on alcohol on the ground, there are none in the air except while flying over Saudi territory. Movies are censored during flight, but no worse than what you would find in North

America. Any hint of nudity will be cut by the censor's scissors, but thankfully, almost all forms of violence are faithfully telecast. Gulf Air is the national carrier of Bahrain. The airline used to be a cooperative carrier operated by four countries, Abu Dhabi, Bahrain, Qatar and Oman. The latter two dropped out leaving Bahrain. Qatar and Oman have their own eponymous airlines and Etihad is the name of the national carrier of Abu Dhabi. Etihad flies direct from Chicago to Abu Dhabi. Royal Jordanian also flies to Amman, where you can get an ongoing flight to Jeddah, Riyadh or Bahrain. Emirates flies the twin deck A-380 from Toronto to Dubai. United Airlines flies from Washington to Bahrain via Kuwait. Currently United is the only North American airline flying anywhere near the Kingdom. If you see American Airlines flights being listed these are only code shares with Gulf Air. Flying from Bahrain to New York on "American Airlines" means flying Gulf Air equipment to London's Terminal I and making a change to Terminal IV. Not much fun, really. Gulf Air does not fly to the Western Hemisphere.

Stopping in Europe on the way to the Gulf is a popular practice. From London there are direct flights to Bahrain and to Riyadh. The same is true for Frankfurt and Paris. You can also fly to Dubai and from there fly on to Bahrain and cross into Saudi by land.

Do not under any circumstances accept a ticket that has you arriving at the King Fahd International Airport in Dammam, unless you have two to three hours to kill on arrival or love standing in line. While the airport is modern, spacious and underused, because of its underuse there are insufficient immigration officers on duty resulting in horrendous waits. If it is your first time in the Kingdom, you will have your picture taken and you will be fingerprinted. All luggage is X-Rayed coming into the Kingdom at an air border.

Do not bring alcohol. It is not permitted to bring a bottle in your bag. You will be punished. The extent of the punishment is anecdotal. Do not expect lashes, but do not expect to walk out into the desert air shortly after arrival either. Imagine if you were caught with marijuana coming into a North American country. There will be grief of one kind or another. The penalty for bringing in unlicensed pharmaceuticals is much, much worse. In Saudi Arabia the penalty for trafficking in drugs is death and the preferred method of execution is beheading.

If you desperately need succor from the opiate family, please wait until you get out of the airport and get to Riyadh. Codeine is sold over the counter under the trade name, "Solpadeine." In Bahrain, codeine is not available over the counter. Steroids can similarly be found in Saudi, but not Bahrain. This is somewhat unusual because in most other respects Saudi is not even in the same league as Bahrain when it comes to permissiveness.

Ground Transportation

Taxis

In both the Kingdom and Bahrain, taxis are in abundant supply. If you are walking the drivers will honk their horns to get your attention. London black cabs, painted white and with left-hand drive, share taxi duties in Bahrain. In the Kingdom, taxis are invariably small Toyotas. Two adults with luggage is at the upper limit of their capacity. Ford Crown Victoria's are sometimes found at airports with even a few minivans.

Traditionally, taxis were quite expensive in Bahrain. The introduction of taxi meters has lowered prices somewhat but beware the driver who does not turn the meter on because "we are brothers" and who tells you "pay what you want." You are not brothers. Insist on the meter. What you want to pay your new-found family member will rarely be enough. The amount your new brother will accept is usually double what the meter would have been.

Buses

Buses are not much used by expats in Saudi or Bahrain. For a Yorks consultant, riding the bus will be seen as an example of eccentric behavior. Worse, it may lead others to the conclusion that Yorks is in serious financial difficulties since its engineers are forced to ride the bus. Saudi Aramco is the exception to this rule. The company maintains a fleet of modern air-conditioned buses which provide services to Saudi Aramco's various work sites. Unfortunately, you can look but you cannot ride: non-employees are not permitted on these Saudi Aramco buses.

Rental Cars

Rental cars are very expensive in the Gulf. You can rent a car with an International driver's license and a credit card, but be prepared to pay. A rental in the Eastern Province or Bahrain will cost you roughly $1000 USD per month. In either country, you will need a letter of authorization to take the car across the international border. While this is a formality, not having the letter in your possession means that you will be turned back at the border. Not to despair: on the Saudi side there is a car service which will deliver you to Bahrain for a mere 200 Saudi riyals. You have to use the car service because crossing the border on foot is not permitted.

Limousine Service

There are car services in Riyadh, the Eastern Province and Bahrain. Hanco will even take you from Riyadh to Bahrain; the one way price is approximately SAR 800. Hanco has an office in Dhahran and services Khobar. In Bahrain, you can contact Hanco at 17321291 or by email, hancoairport@gmail.com. In Khobar the number is 03894 8441.

Buying a Car

You will soon tire of taking taxis and trying to communicate with those who up until recently knew only the Pashtun-speaking areas of Pakistan and decide that you need your own transportation.

Resist the temptation to purchase a vehicle immediately. If you are a new employee, you have a ninety-day probationary period to get through, and during this time you can be let go for any reason. If you are a Yorks transferee, you may decide, sooner than you would have thought, that Saudi Arabia is not for you and you do not want to be burdened with an automobile along with all of the rest of your problems. After your probationary period is up you may decide to purchase a used vehicle which you can sell back into the market when you leave.

In addition to newspaper classifieds, there is a lemon lot by the Al Jazeera Supermarket in Juffair as well as newspaper classifieds. Both Saco stores and Tamimi Supermarkets in Saudi Arabia have bulletin boards where you can check used car ads. Saudi Aramco has a corporate Intranet with a very active used car market; unfortunately you do not have access.

There is an active used car market amongst the employees of Saudi Aramco but you will not have access to their electronic bulletin board. If you can obtain access, it is probably the best place to find used cars in the Kingdom. The government of Bahrain has announced that it will begin removing cars displaying "For Sale" signs from streets and lemon lots around the capital. This action is being touted as a safety and security measure but in fact was requested by more traditional used car dealerships as an anti-competitive measure. Vehicles will be towed and owners will have to pay 200 BD to recover them. The last crackdown was in 2008, so if when you arrive the lemon lots are half-empty rest assured that over time enforcement will wane and the lots will invariably fill up again with product.

If you are going to be crossing the international border on a daily basis you should spend a little more to lessen the chance of mechanical problems stranding you in the no man's land between two countries. Whether you will be able to purchase a vehicle depends to some extent on your status in either country. You cannot purchase a vehicle in Saudi Arabia without an *iqama* and you cannot purchase a vehicle in Bahrain without a CPR. If Yorks gets a CPR for you in Bahrain you will have no difficulty; otherwise expect problems in registering the vehicle and obtaining insurance every year. This is another reason why rentals are both expensive and popular.

Currency

Saudi currency is accepted in Bahrain but not vice-versa. In the Eastern Province you may find that the larger establishments will take Bahraini currency–Ikea does–but except for Ikea, Saudi establishments are usually not happy about doing so and will charge you for their inconvenience.

Dress Code

In public, all women are required to wear an *abaya*, a loose-fitting black gown. Saudi women usually cover their hair. Some foreign women cover their hair, but this is not a requirement. Similarly, some women are veiled but not all. There are different kinds of veil ranging from a light black cloth which completely covers the face to the *niqab*, which covers the nose and mouth but not the eyes. Women of different nationalities approach the dress code on a generalized basis, though as with everything else, there are exceptions. Very conservative religious women will wear black gloves in public as well. Some women find this dress code to be conveniently protective; one woman wrote of putting on a *niqab* for safety from the unwanted stares of men, wearing it "like a crash helmet." The *abaya* has a similar function.

Saudi men wear the *thobe*, a cassock-like garment which reaches the floor. The *thobe* is almost always white, except in winter when it can be different colored, even black. Saudi men wear a skullcap which is covered by red and white headress called a *shemagh*. Two interlocked black bands, called a *ghutra*, are placed around the head keep the *shemagh* in place. The very religious do not use the *ghutra*.

One stylistic detail that Hollywood almost always gets wrong is that the *shemagh* has one fold, and only one fold, which peaks on a line in the middle of the face. In Bahrain, the *shemagh* will usually be white instead of red and white. Over the thobe and especially in cold weather, the men wear a *bissht*, a brown colored robe which appears to have gold threads. A thinner version is worn on formal occasions in any weather. The threads are not actually gold–this is forbidden–but are actually gold-colored silver.

Hotel

If you are going to be working in Al Khobar, Yorks will move heaven and earth to make sure that you do not spend any time in Bahrain. The reason for this is that there is a fear that you will like Bahrain so much that you will refuse to stay in Khobar or ask for a transfer.

A fair interpretation is that living and working in Khobar is viewed as punishment compared to Bahrain. You will hear half-uttered comments and jokes from time to time threatening to transfer one of the Bahrain-based consultants to Khobar if billings do not improve or if they are not kept at an appropriately high level. If management believes that working in Khobar is punishment, perhaps it would be best to believe them. After all, there must be a reason for their belief.

In some cases, a new arrival is taken directly from the airport in Bahrain to Al Khobar without passing Go or picking up two hundred dollars. If this is not feasible, you will be taken early the next morning to Saudi Arabia. In Khobar, more likely than not, you will stay at the Mövenpick Hotel. The hotel is relatively close to the office though walking is not possible. Taxi service from the hotel is spotty so your best bet is to pick up a taxi that has left guests at the hotel. Ground Transportation!TaxisOtherwise you will have to wait. And wait. And wait some more. When the driver finally arrives he will be unhappy that he is being forced to navigate through a construction zone and that because of the relatively short distance, he is going to receive only a paltry sum for his trouble.

There is an advantage to putting a hotel in an isolated area. As a new arrival, you are as of yet unaccustomed to the calls for prayer. The sixth and the only optional call to prayer, *Dhuha*, comes at dawn. In time, you will soon learn to sleep through the call. Meanwhile, it is unlikely you will hear the call at the Movenpick. The Mövenpick in Khobar is like any four star hotel kept to international standards anywhere in the world except that it is not. At first you will notice only subtle hints welcoming you to the new reality. The minibar is full but there is no alcohol. Do not bother asking for the hotel bar because there isn't one. There is an unusual sticker on the wall with an arrow pointing to the *qibla*, with which you are as of yet unfamiliar. The Bible has not been left by the Gideons in the nightstand and even if you were to say at the flagship Marriott in Riyadh, you would not find the Book of Mormon. Instead you will find a copy of the Qu'ran, in Arabic, printed in Saudi Arabia. Women in black robes sit in the hotel lobby. But they are not nuns. Other than that, you could be anywhere in the world.

There is a Mövenpick in Bahrain as well.

The *qibla*, by the way, is the direction the Faithful must turn towards in prayer, the House of God in Mecca.

One Office to Rule them All

One Office, Two Locations

York's policy is that in the Gulf there is "one office, two locations." Do not let the tendency to trust lead you to accept this pronouncement. Yorks has two offices in the Gulf and the employees in each are treated differently. There are many good consultants and there are many consultants who can tolerate Saudi Arabia but there are few good consultants who can tolerate Saudi Arabia. I know of only one consultant who marveled at the openness, the many dining options and the abundance of water in the Kingdom. However, before coming to Riyadh he had spent six months underwater on patrol in a U.S. Navy submarine.

The diplomatic services of many countries classify Saudi Arabia as a hardship post. There is a reason for this.

Bahrain Office

The Bahrain office is located in the Big Office Building near the historic *Baab Al-Bahrain* area in the center of Manama.

Near the complex is the home to the Capital Club. Yorks has a corporate membership there and it is an excellent place to take clients because of its amenities, bar and spectacular view of the city from the 52nd floor. But it is not for you. Though club rules and the terms of Yorks corporate membership permit adding associates as members without paying an initiation fee, Yorks will neither pay for your membership nor put your name forward so that you can pay for your own. The Capital Club is discussed in more detail in the section titled, "Miscellaneous."

There is a taxi stand in front of the *Baab Al-Bahrain*, the Bahrain Gate, and the old center of town. To get there you have to cross ten lanes of traffic so the walk can be somewhat perilous. There is a functioning traffic light to stop traffic but you dawdle at your own risk. The Intercontinental Hotel is on the other side of the highway along with more economical two and three star alternatives, though some of these are off-limits to Navy personnel because of bad behavior engaged in by residents and guests. Unlike Khobar, the area of the Bahrain office is well known to taxi drivers.

Khobar Office

The Al Khobar office is in the Remote Office Building on the Dammam-Khobar Coastal Road. Repairs to the sole access road are entering their second year with no end in sight. Roads are being ripped up in front of the building and for several kilometers in either direction. The work was in progress in June, 2012 and while a good deal of progress has been made the road appears to have been built with some of the lanes or roadways on different levels. Equalizing them will likely take another two years or so. This makes getting to and from the Khobar office a nightmare not just for Yorks personnel but for clients as well. There is a cafeteria in the building that is open for lunch. There are no vending machines or other stores of any kind and nothing within walking distance. There is a Dunkin' Donuts five minutes away, but to get there driving times may be doubled or tripled due to the construction. There is no public transportation to the office and Khobar taxi drivers are unfamiliar with its location. When leaving the building no taxis are available and a car will have to be summoned. Here are the phone numbers of several car services in Khobar:

Al Gosaibi 3857 7711
Hala Limousine 3858 1100
Hanco Limousine 3894 8441
Majestic(Aramco) 3876 8881
Samara Limousine 3891 1500

Work Week

In Saudi, Saturday is always Monday and Friday is Sunday. In Bahrain, Sunday is Monday and Saturday is Sunday.

In Saudi, your weekend consists of one day—Friday—because in the private sector it is customary to work a half day on Thursday. Government offices, however, close on Wednesday and do not reopen until Saturday morning. The problem is that since the Yorks Khobar office is in a government building all of the facilities are closed on Thursday and Friday. Getting in out of the building on Thursdays can be difficult. In Bahrain, there is a two day weekend on Friday and Saturday.

Because many of your clients will be Western companies they will expect you to be reachable on both Thursdays and Fridays. So in a practical sense, there is no weekend in Saudi at all. Bahrain at least shares one day of the weekend, Saturday, with the West.

[*Publisher's Note: In 2013, the Saudi weekend was harmonized with the rest of the GCC. Government workers are given Friday and Saturday off. The private sector now takes Friday off and Saturday becomes either a half day or a full day off. Saudi Aramco follows the government schedule so that Friday and Saturday are now the weekend.*]

Hours

Traditionally Saudi offices opened at 0930 and closed at 1:30 for siesta and reopened at 1700 until 2100. The new tendency, even in conservative Riyadh, is for a single shift. In the Eastern Province two shifts are less prevalent and the single shift is what you will normally encounter. Yorks in Khobar does not close for siesta. Office hours in Khobar are 0830 to 1700. Working from home is a disfavored Western innovation in Saudi Arabia and it makes no difference if your employer is a Western company. It is assumed that if you are not in the office you are not working.

If you do not have an access card you will not be able to enter the building before 0830. If you are still in the office after five, you can get out but by then the electronic locks will have engaged on the doors to the office and the building. There is a button to the immediate right of the door of the office. Press it and when you hear the lock disengage, push to open. The lock deactivator for the building's main doors is harder to find. Face the building's main doors which face the highway perpetually under construction. To the left you will see a plant; behind it is a button about a meter or so off the ground. Press it and move quickly to the door. If you are not agile enough to get out before the locks re-engage or if the lock deactivator does not work, you can take the stairs to the basement.

The garage doors will open from the inside using a switch and the door at the bottom of the emergency exit stairs opens manually from the inside with a push. The garage doors normally require a key card to operate but if you do not have one, you can open the doors by pushing a switch near the door frame.

Getting out of the building at night can be challenging. There is probably a hidden meaning behind this fact.

Dress Code

According to the Yorks unfinished Gulf employee manual, Wednesday is casual dress day in Al Khobar. This has not been implemented because Wednesday is a regular work day in Saudi Arabia and the concept of "casual" dress has not caught on in a land where half wear white and half wear black. Casual day is really only observed on Thursdays, which at least in theory should be the weekend. In Bahrain, Thursday is casual day which means that jeans can be worn to the office.

Government Offices

Government offices in the Kingdom are open from 0730 to 1430 and from Saturday to Wednesday.

Driving

You do not know how to drive. You only think that you do. The Kingdom has one of the highest road accident rates in the world. Official statistics show that 9 million traffic accidents annually cause SR 13 billion in damages. There are 18 deaths per day which works out to one traffic death every ninety minutes. Driving in Saudi Arabia is unlike anything you have ever experienced behind the wheel.

The traffic laws are for the most part cosmetic. The police have traditionally shied away from enforcing them because in a country that has roughly eighteen principal tribal groups, the odds of being related to an offender is uncomfortably high. Either that or the police have better things to do. In the unlikely event you are stopped, you will be required to produce the vehicle's registration, called the *istmara*, as well as a driver's license and proof of insurance.

In the absence of enforcement, traffic is essentially chaos. Rules are for others. After driving for a while in Saudi Arabia you will see possible passing lanes where there were none before; the word "shoulder" becomes meaningless and who said it's unlawful to pass on a one-lane exit ramp?

Making a left-hand turn from the left lane is so limiting. That is why on a multi-lane road left hand turns can and are made from any lane. This is sometimes called the "Saudi Sweep." This eliminates the worry about getting in the correct lane in preparation for a turn. With respect to the right lane, it is "Go" at all times. There is no such thing as a right turn on red–that is, there will be right turns on red, green or yellow–the color of the traffic signal does not matter as the right lane is functionally exempt from any traffic control restriction.

You will not be lonely while driving in the Kingdom. A glance in the rear-view mirror will usually reveal someone tailgating you as if looking for a slingshot in the Daytona 500 NASCAR race. The fact that you are already well over the speed limit (when in Rome, after all) is of no significance.

I used to own an old car and from time to time I would have to visit a junkyard in the United States in order to find parts. In that junkyard there were many cars that only a few that stood as witnesses to a horrible crash. Visiting a Saudi junkyard is not a pleasant experience. In Saudi Arabia, it seems that every wreck in the junkyard is a death car; one car after another is a cenotaph.

Out of frustration, the government recently introduced the *saher* (sentinel) system to increase compliance with traffic rules. The system consists of radar and camera -quipped semi-armored vehicles, usually SUV's, parked at places which either a) have been the scene of a horrible accident; or b) is a place where violations are likely to have been committed. In short, the entire country. From time to time maintenance comes by and picks up the cameras if the cars have survived the rocks that Saudis tend to throw at them. If you commit a traffic violation that is recorded on the system, you will get a text message shortly afterward inviting you to come in and pay the fine.

Because of the combination of large families—one of the consequences of polygamy and low gasoline prices—large cars are ubiquitous in Saudi Arabia. These large SUV's, often seen packed with wives and children, are no more likely to respect traffic laws than a teenager on a moped. An unusual local custom is leaving the dealer sticker on the car window long after purchase. Even though a car may be two or three years old, the presence of the sticker on the window allows the owner to claim that the vehicle is "new." For the same reason the plastic coverings protecting car seats during vehicle shipping are similarly not removed. Sometimes you might even see plastic or rubber bump guards installed on car doors for ocean voyages remaining long after the car has driven off the ship.

Gasoline is cheaper than water. The cheapest grade costs 45 halalas per liter; the expensive grade is 60 halalas per liter. There are one hundred halalas to a riyal, and 3.75 riyals to the U.S. Dollar. One liter is .0264 gallons and one gallon equals 3.875 liters. 3.875 x 45 = 170.325 halalas or 1.7 riyals. This means that a gallon of gasoline in Saudi Arabia will cost either 45 cents or 60 cents. Feel free to check the math.

Traffic signs are bilingual, English/Arabic. Usually. Surprisingly, this is more the case outside Riyadh than inside Riyadh. For some strange reason, the signs in the Diplomatic Quarter in Riyadh, home to many non-Arabic speaking foreigners, are almost exclusively Arabic only.

Because of the climate extremes, systemic mechanical breakdowns often first manifest themselves in Saudi Arabia. Tread separation issues with Firestone 500 tires, and horrific Ferrari engine fires were first seen in the Kingdom. The common thread is the heat, which can reach 50 degrees centigrade in the summer. The Saudi Arabic word for water is *moya*. A different word is used in Modern Standard Arabic (*ma*). Here, use *moya*. Keep this in mind if you find yourself stranded in the desert with a steaming radiator, for few experiences can beat the excitement of riding back to Riyadh in a flat bed truck ahead of your car with a blown-out overheated engine after a failed escape run to Bahrain.

Police checkpoints are common features of Saudi highways and may be thrown up anywhere. A checkpoint may be fixed or it may simply appear out of nowhere. Between Riyadh and Al Khobar there are at least three more or less permanent checkpoints. You often cannot tell if a traffic slowdown is due to a horrific accident or merely a checkpoint. If you are a Westerner, more often than not, you will be waived through. But not always. Sometimes desperate souls try to smuggle liquor to Riyadh from Bahrain and every now and then get caught.

Normally you will not see too many "No Parking" signs in the Kingdom and the ones you do see can safely be ignored. For all intents and purposes parking tickets are unknown and there are no tow trucks hunting illegally parked cars on the streets. In Bahrain, your vehicle may be ticketed if illegally parked in the Diplomatic Quarter and your car risks be towed if parked on an empty lot while displaying a "For Sale" sign.

The real danger is parking near someone's home. It does not matter that you are on the public way and not blocking the driveway or entrance. Saudis do not like people parking near their homes, even if no one is being bothered. The standard Saudi response to this unwelcome behavior is to let almost all of the air out of one tire. When this happens, you will have to limp to a gas station for air or a new tire. This is the kind of information you will not find in guidebooks but which you need to know.

Women are not permitted to drive in Saudi Arabia. This is a rule that everyone knows about and there is no lack of opinions on the issue. Keep in mind that while women are not permitted to drive automobiles they can be licensed to fly airplanes or drive trains. At Princess Noura University in Riyadh, all of the train operators are women.

In Bahrain, women are permitted to drive automobiles. If seeing a woman behind the wheel of an automobile appears strange to you, it is time to take home leave.

Crossing the Border

Crossing the border from Saudi Arabia to Bahrain is not difficult but it is helpful to know what to expect before you try.

First, you must be sure that your Saudi visa allows you to exit. If you have overstayed your visa the SAR 10,000 fine will be imposed, the penalty will not be waived and arrangements cannot be made at the border. Yorks will not reimburse you for the cost unless you have received a specific order to overstay your visa. Otherwise, it is your responsibility to stay on top of your exit and entry dates.

If you do not have a multiple exit/entry visa when you exit it will be a one-way trip. If you have an *iqama*, remember that your permission to enter and leave the country lasts for only one year and must be renewed. If your permission has expired you will be turned back. No amount of pleading will work at the border, or for that matter, anywhere else.

Assuming that you have a proper multiple exit/entry visa your next consideration is transportation. If you have a car with Saudi license plates, you will need permission to take the car across the border. Obtaining permission takes about a day. You need a company letter stamped at the Chamber of Commerce. If your car is in your own name you may still need a company letter though the rules change from time to time.

If you do not have the proper permission to take the car out of the country, do not even try to do so. If you try you will be turned back. However, all is not lost–there are alternatives. There is a parking lot on the Saudi side of the border and you can leave the car there. If you decide not to ever come back to Saudi Arabia, at least have the courtesy to advise the car rental company where their vehicle has been abandoned so they can pick it up. If you drive and leave the car on the Saudi side of the border you can take a taxi which will take you across and into Manama. For many years the rate has been SR 200 each way. In the parking lot Saudi men loiter offering informal taxi service through customs and into Bahrain. Prices are negotiable but usually cost less than taxi service. Be prepared to bargain.

There is also public transportation. Saptco buses leave from Olaya Street in Riyadh and after stopping in Al Khobar cross to Bahrain. Their station in Manama is near the Central Market. The cost of the trip is SR 200. This is the sole instance when you may ride the bus in the Kingdom.

Otherwise, follow the road signs to Bahrain. The causeway is 26 kilometers long and an island sits at the halfway point. When you reach the causeway, you will have to pay a toll costing SR 20 or BD 2. You can also pay in Qatari or Emirati currency if you like. If you need change, make sure that the change you are given is not Qatari or Emirati because neither currency is accepted anywhere in Saudi Arabia or Bahrain.

After entering the Causeway, you will drive thirteen kilometers to an artificial island that sits on top of the international border. On the Saudi side there are several fast food restaurants, a mosque, the aforementioned taxi service, a restaurant on top of a tower (colored green) with a view of the Bahraini side and a parking lot. The parking lot fills up on weekends but there is overflow parking on the island. Depending how crowded things are you might have to be a little creative when it comes time to park your car.

Just before the main parking area surrounded by shops there is a left-hand turn lane with a sign saying "Diplomats." If you have the good fortune to have a diplomatic passport, you can turn left here and breeze through customs formalities. Even if you are not a diplomat, for SR 10,000 you can acquire a VIP pass that will let you drive back and forth quickly. If you dream that Yorks will reimburse you for this expense to facilitate your cross-border travel pinch yourself because you are, well, dreaming.

At this point you can turn back and drive back across the causeway to Khobar or you can continue on to Bahrain. The first checkpoint is Saudi customs. They will verify that you have the proper permission to take your car across the border and will issue you a cash register size receipt. Hold onto this receipt, it will be examined several times during your journey across the border. There is no other Saudi customs inspection upon leaving the country. Usually getting through the first checkpoint is fairly quick.

After obtaining the receipt, the next checkpoint, about 250 meters away, is Saudi passport control. Though there are multiple lanes, this is the biggest choke point of all. The waits here are interminable. Complicating matters is that the traffic lines up in lines behind each booth displaying a green traffic light signal. When the light turns from red to green, signifying the opening of a new booth, traffic will tear out of line at a high rate of speed to make it over to a new booth. Given that lanes are usually ignored when driving in Saudi Arabia, the chaos here is only increased by desperate drivers trying to obtain slight advantage over each other.

At the Saudi passport checkpoint it is a good idea to hold your passport open to your Saudi visa page. You will need to hand over your customs receipt as well. Both will be stamped and you can continue on.

If there is a problem with your paperwork you will be asked to leave your car just past the booth and you will be directed to the office building in the center of the roadway. Inside, immigration officers will try and determine the nature of the problem, but often there is no problem at all and you will simply be directed to return to the booth so you can proceed.

After passing through Saudi immigration, there is another checkpoint about 250 meters away. Here you normally–but not always–drive at slow speed through while holding up the newly-stamped customs receipt to an officer sitting in another booth. After you pass this checkpoint, you have now completed Saudi formalities and the Bahraini part of the process will commence..

The first Bahraini checkpoint, about 500 meters away, is Bahraini immigration. Unlike Saudi immigration, the Bahraini process is usually much quicker. If you do not have a Bahraini visa you will have to pay SR 50 (BD 5). The visa is valid for thirty days. If you are flying out the same day from Bahrain (and can show a plane ticket) you should not have to pay anything at all. The Bahraini immigration officer will not need your Saudi customs receipt but hold on to it nonetheless.

Bahraini customs is the next stop after Bahraini immigration. At peak periods there are two lanes–one on the right and one on the left. The one on the left is usually quicker–the drivers are not always asked to get out of their cars and are often waved through. On the right side, which is the only lane open at non-peak times, you will probably be required to stop your car and open the trunk.

After the customs inspection, there is the final checkpoint about 100 meters away. If you have an automobile with Bahraini plates it is already insured. Drive all the way to the left and line up at the booth marked, "Insured Vehicles." When you reach your turn at the booth you will turn in the stamped Saudi customs receipt.

If your car has Saudi (or other) plates, drive to the right and line up at any of the multiple booths marked "Non-insured Vehicles." You must purchase liability insurance coverage for as long as you plan to stay in Bahrain.

After passing this final insurance checkpoint you are now officially in Bahrain. On the Bahraini side there is a police station, a mysterious McDonald's restaurant sign (mysterious because there is no McDonald's on the Bahraini side of the island) and an identical tower topped by a Bahraini flag and a restaurant from which you can peer into Saudi Arabia. The neon lights on the tower at night are red instead of green.

The restaurant on the Bahraini side tends to be busier because Western tourists who don't have Saudi visas come to peer into the Kingdom. This is as close as they will get. In 1979 the British travel writer Jonathan Raban published a book called *Arabia: Through the Looking Glass*. While Raban visited every other country on the Arabian peninsual, without a Saudi visa he could only look from this restaurant across the waters.

After you pass the insurance checkpoint, you will find a single traffic light. Past the traffic light you are off the island and the causeway continues across the Arabian Gulf into northwestern Bahrain.

Entering Saudi Arabia from Bahrain is essentially the same procedure in reverse but there are a few differences. You must purchase Saudi insurance for your Bahraini vehicle before you reach the causeway as Bahraini insurance is not valid in Saudi Arabia and there is no final insurance checkpoint on the Saudi side. Before you reach the Causeway, look for the sign which says "Insurance." Unfortunately, it is easy to miss. If you enter the first queue without a valid policy, you will be directed to return because you cannot bring a car into the Kingdom on your standard Bahraini insurance policy. To buy insurance you will see three lanes after exiting with tollbooths where Saudi insurance is sold. At least one is open 24 hours per day. You can buy liability insurance there at the rate of BD 1.5 per day. Buying on a monthly basis is cheaper. Consider buying comprehensive insurance as petty crime in Saudi Arabia is unfortunately on the rise. You will be given a receipt here.

After you enter the Causeway, you drive to the island where the first stop is Bahraini Customs. You usually are asked to show the insurance receipt and permission letter to take the car into Saudi Arabia, but sometimes you are just given a customs receipt and no documents are reviewed. You will need this paper at Bahraini immigration, the next stop. After going through Bahraini immigration there is a final stop on the Bahraini side which is not always manned. Driving on, the next checkpoint is Saudi passports and again this is the site of the longest delays. If it is your first visit to Saudi Arabia you will have to wait in line in your automobile and then when you reach the booth you will be directed to leave your car and go to the office building. There you will be fingerprinted and your photograph will be taken.

After having your passport stamped at Saudi immigration, the next step is Saudi customs. Here every single vehicle will be inspected and the customs receipt you were given by Bahraini customs stamped. Afterwards, there is a final checkpoint. It used to be that you simply handed the stamped receipt to the officer and drove through, but now the officers are entering the receipt's number into a computer, causing further delay.

There is no further insurance checkpoint on the Saudi side. Coming out of the last checkpoint you will find yourself at a partial traffic circle that borders the parking lot. There is a McDonald's sign here as well, but surprisingly—compared to the Bahraini side—this sign is accompanied by a restaurant.

Completing all these formalities during non-peak hours is normally efficient and can be accomplished in an hour or less. At peak times it can be an absolute, chaotic nightmare. Thursday afternoons are particularly bad as the traffic lines fill with Saudis who want to spend their weekend in Bahrain. Similarly, on Saturday afternoons the lines for returning to the Kingdom are just as bad. It can take up to three hours to cross at these times.

Imagine having to run this gauntlet each way every day and you will have some idea of the sufferings of those who live in Bahrain and work in Saudi.

Housing

Saudi labor regulations require the employer to provide the employee with housing as well as transportation. For employers with many expatriate employees, the phenomena of the compound has sprung up to meet this legal requirement. Compounds are gated communities where sometimes harsh Saudi laws are relaxed. Inside, women do not have to wear the *abaya*, gender segregation is largely ignored and Western pastimes, such as daily drinking, are tolerated. Compound accommodations are quite expensive and Saudi landlords require payment of a year's rent in advance. Since 2006, licensed foreign enterprises have been given the right to acquire land in their own name for the purpose of housing their own employees, but in practice permission is rarely granted.

For non-Canadian employees at least, Yorks in the Gulf is no different. Yorks leased a corporate apartment from a Sudanese landlord in Ireland, that great home of Sudanese emigration. The apartment overlooks the site of the former Pearl (now GCC) Roundabout, Ground Zero for the protests against the government which sprang up as part of the Arab Spring in early 2011. To get to the apartment today requires passing through several checkpoints as the entire area remains under military occupation. Nevertheless, the apartment building is pleasant and the apartment itself has all of the amenities. There is a grocery store on the ground floor. In case of a state of siege or the imposition of a general curfew, the apartment would be a fine perch from which to weather the civil storm. Unfortunately, the lease was permitted to lapse. I am told that a new apartment is being sought, but whether this is true or not, I do not know.

In Khobar, Yorks has nothing.

Non-Canadian employees are essentially on their own. Not too long ago, we had at least four months notice that a recent hire was on his way but no one took any steps to make sure that he had reasonable accommodations. He was on his own, as you will be. If it takes a month to find a place, take a month. It is a good idea to investigate all of the possibilities in person. The pressure of daily hotel bills may even cause those with the power to remedy the situation to do so.

Also keep in mind that once you move out of the hotel you will be paying for your accommodations out of your own pocket. While this is standard in North America (except at work camps) it is not the practice in Saudi Arabia. Nevertheless, Yorks has adopted the practice so govern yourself accordingly.

Housing at Saudi Aramco in Dhahran

You may have heard favorable things about the Aramco compound. In Dhahran there is a vibrant, active community with full services, restaurants, a golf course, a bowling alley, swimming pools, horseback riding and even accommodations for single women. Due to widespread irrigation and landscaping, living on the Aramco compound in Dharan does not feel like living in Saudi Arabia at all. Like Century City in South Florida, many people living on the compound get around not by car, but by golf cart. It is a friendly place.

Unfortunately, it has nothing to do with you. I was told when I arrived in Khobar that it was possible to get by inexpensively by house sitting on the Aramco compound. This is not true. Unless you are an Aramco employee or a contractor with status, you cannot even enter the compound without an invitation and, to one former Yorks Gulf consultant's chagrin, having grown up on the compound makes absolutely no difference. For Yorks employees, the possibility of living on the Aramco compound does not exist.

Getting inside the Aramco compound is no simple matter. Normally there are three checkpoints that must be navigated before one arrives on the compound. There may be a temporary traffic stop like those often thrown up on any road in Saudi, usually consisting of two or three police cars positioned to funnel traffic down to one lane. Further down the road there is a semi-permanent checkpoint guarded by a tent-like structure, and further along still there is a permanent gate where individuals without Aramco credentials are challenged. Assuming that you can convince the guards that there is a reason for your presence, you can enter Aramco's outer area where there are offices, a grocery store, car rental facilities and a museum. You can even drive by Prosperity Well, the first producing oil well dug by Aramco in the Kingdom—it is still a working well and the oil still flows.

To enter the residential areas there is a final permanent checkpoint and to pass this one you have to get out of your car and enter a building where your identification will be checked and the person you wish to visit will be called—on a landline. The guard will listen in to the conversation to make sure that you know each other, and then and only then will you be given a pass to enter. If the conversation takes place in a language other than English or Arabic, the guard will look at you strangely but he will continue to listen because that is what he has been told to do.

Living on the Aramco compound in Dhahran is not a solution to the problem of housing Yorks employees in Saudi Arabia. If you think that you can somehow finagle a house share or even formal accommodations on the Aramco compound, you are wrong. The sooner you forget about these ideas, the better.

Curiously, official Saudi Aramco contractors, are given access, accommodations and compound credentials for their employees who are visiting the Kingdom for short and medium term projects. Yorks does not have access to such benefits. Any information you have to the contrary is aspirational thinking.

Employee Housing in Saudi Arabia

Compounds in the Eastern Province are the only attractive choice if you are going to avoid the commute and live in the Kingdom. Unfortunately, there is a general housing shortage and currently there are no vacancies. Your employer should have put you on the waiting list well in advance of your arrival. Unfortunately, he has not done so and now that you have arrived it is too late. No Canadians working for Yorks are living in Saudi Arabia so there is no reason why (that is, if you hold a Canadian passport) you cannot demand to be provided housing (or a housing allowance) in Bahrain as well as having Manama designated as your work location. Otherwise, you are out of luck.

If you do find a place in the Eastern Province it can only

be rented on an annual basis. Unlike most real estate leases, in Saudi Arabia rent must be paid in full in cash for the entire period at the commencement of the lease. That means, cash up front. Usually, there is no other alternative. Good luck.

Housing in Bahrain

Even though Bahrain is tiny compared to the size of Saudi Arabia, the Bahraini housing market has little in common with the Big Kingdom. Comfortable accommodations are plentiful and furnished apartments can be rented on a daily, weekly or monthly basis. There are several real estate agents who have assisted the firm in the past to find villas (i.e., houses) for employees with families. While there are real estate agents in the Eastern Province, they seem to be less accessible than their colleagues in Bahrain. Perhaps this is because there is less inventory for them to market. It may also be because there are restrictions on foreigners entering the real estate market.

Finding a place to live in Bahrain is not a difficult task. The only complication is the time you will need to take from the office to visit all the different alternatives in order to make an informed choice.

Even though it is possible to live in Bahrain and commute to Saudi Arabia the official Yorks policy is that Khobar-based consultants must live in Saudi Arabia. Were they not to do so, it would be more difficult to treat them differently from the employees whose offices are in the Yorks Bahrain location. Khobar employees are actively–though fruitlessly–kept away from Bahrain as much as possible. This will become an element of serious friction with your employer. Though it seems trivial–

after all, as long as you complete your work what difference does it make where you live?–this issue consumes many in the office. You would think there is nothing else more serious to worry about.

Electricity

Saudi Arabia

Electrical current standards in Saudi Arabia have not been standardized. Electrical current in the Eastern Province is normally provided at 110 volts except when it is not. In Riyadh you are more likely to find 220 volts. Except for all those times when you find 110. You may find North American flat prong, European round pin and U.K. fused plugs side by side. The wall outlet may provide 110, 220 or even 440 volts.

Resist the temptation of assuming that because an outlet accepts flat prongs that it necessarily is supplying 110 volts. It may be, or it may not. Similarly, the fact that an appliance has flat prongs does not necessarily mean that it uses 110 volts. Appliances in stores are available in 110 or 220 volt models so examine the packaging closely before purchase. Locals usually purchase a voltage tester to verify what is actually flowing through a particular electrical outlet. A china marker or a grease pencil should be used to mark the outlets. A houseguest's failure to pay attention to such matters resulted in a burned-out microwave.So trust, but verify.

There is a difference between a plug converter and a transformer. A plug converter will simply allow you to adapt your plug to the outlet at hand, assuming that the outlet meets your power requirements. In the West, you may have seen these adapters in stores supplying travel goods or selling suitcases. In Saudi Arabia they are sold in grocery stores (Tamimi/Safeway) Panda and Carrefour, and Saco, the hardware store. Australian angled plugs and thick pin South African plugs are available as well. Sometimes you will come across the phenomenon of an appliance with the plug removed and the insulation stripped exposing bare wires that can be inserted into a wall outlet directly, avoiding the inconvenience of finding a compatible plug completely. If you insist on connecting such a modified-plug appliance, at least wear rubber gloves while doing so and make sure your employer-provided life insurance is paid and the policy up to date.

Power transformers are widely available and provide 110 volt power supplies on a 220 outlet or vice versa. Some transformers provide both power sources. Transformers are fused so if you exceed the rated level of the transformer the fuse will blow (and you will have to purchase a new one) and the power will go out. This is particularly a problem with laser printers and hair dryers. Retail transformers for sale in Saudi Arabia use automobile fuses (Littelfuse) and do not have a flipped switch that can be restored to a working position. Transformers can make mechanical scraping noises that will initially be unfamiliar to you. If you are in an office and there appears to be a good deal of random scraping sounds, transformers are probably being used.

In spite of the spaghetti tangle of wires connecting pole to building, the power grid in Saudi Arabia is remarkably reliable. Blackouts and brown-outs are not common and few buildings other than hospitals have their own generator.

There can be localized exceptions. In June of 2004 I had the misfortune of living in a building that housed several Westerners and had no special security of its own. Al-Qaeda in the Arabian Peninsula had become active in Malaz in Riyadh and had beheaded two Westerners. Before the organization's leader was killed in a police shoot-out, things were looking very dicey. One evening, the power went out in the building. I looked outside expecting a brown-out such as you might see in tropical countries or cities with a third-world infrastructure, like Miami. Instead, the street lights shone brightly and the only building on the block without power was ours. "This is when they come to kill us," I thought, but nothing happened. The next day–you don't seriously think the problem would be solved that evening, do you?–an electrocuted rat was found near the mains that connected the building to the grid. The rat had gnawed on the wires and his efforts took out the power to the building. So if there is an unannounced, unscheduled power outage a rodent may be responsible. In that case, taping the toilets might help prevent a repeat occurrence.

The subject of electricity in an employee manual would rarely require more than a sentence or two for most countries, but Saudi Arabia is not like most countries.

Bahrain

Electricity in Bahrain is supplied at 220 volts and fused, three-pronged U.K. plugs are used.

Wasn't that easy?

Water

In the desert that is Saudi Arabia, water is a major issue. Before the advent of Islam, shari'a referred to the path to water. Tap water in Riyadh is recycled and desalinated through osmosis. Cisterns are often on the roofs of buildings and while water pressure is often weak, the lack of pressure is not usually a problem. Nevertheless, a low water pressure shower head is a wise investment. There are municipal sewers and a municipal water supply but some areas of the city—and this is particularly a problem in Jeddah—depend on water trucks for delivery.

You may have heard of the "Riyadh River." Do not be confused into thinking that this waterway is the source of Riyadh's drinking water. This stream (if you can call it that) is not a river at all but the directed flow of chlorinated and processed sewage. It is dumped for irrigation in the desert not far from Riyadh. It is amazing to see the greenery that has grown up around the sluices and the river itself. Though far from the rain forest, there is a certain tropical feel to the area, scented by the fragrance of chlorine. But be thankful: viruses and bacteria cannot survive in the presence of chlorine.

If your water runs out there will be no bathing. Expect this to happen every two months or so. When this happens, there may be enough water in the system to take a sponge bath before the taps run completely dry.

Bathing in Saudi Arabia can be a challenge for other reasons. The first problem is figuring out the purpose of the three taps. There is one tap for hot water, another for cold water and the third one is for what exactly? The placement of the third tap may be out of the way and the hot and cold taps may be combined. The third tap is not for the drain, it is a master (or sub-master) control valve that turns the water on and off. Do not presume that the third tap turns off all water to the bathroom entirely. While this is possible, usually it will only be for the shower. You may also find such a third tap in the kitchen and another wherever you have a water heater.

Unfortunately, bathrooms do not come with instruction manuals and the trial and error method when there are three taps can be complicated if you leap to the erroneous conclusion that the third tap has something to do with hot water. It does not. The hot water heater is usually controlled by an additional light switch found somewhere in the bathroom or just outside and which you have already ignored because turning it on and off appeared to do nothing.

Toilets always come with a spritzer (called a *shouf*) for personal hygiene. Its careless use may explain the water stains on the bathroom's ceiling. Following the European, rather than the North American practice, bidets are also nearly universal. Even in a males-only environment, bidets are useful for the ritual washing of feet (*wudu*) which is a recommended prerequisite to prayer.

Water tanks are often exposed to direct sunlight. This, combined with desert conditions and the extreme heat of the summer, means that during the day there is no cold water to mediate the temperature. So if you need to take a shower after 10:00 am you may not be able to do so without suffering first degree burns. The previously-mentioned low water pressure shower head outputs a steam-like spray that is more tolerable. In the late evening things get back to normal. Of course, what you think is normal is not necessarily normal here. An unexpected advantage of this difficulty in regulating heat in the summer is that the water from the tap is hot enough to cook soup.

If you find that the soup you are making has unusual or somewhat unexpected flavors, it is a good idea to check the cistern. If your landlord in Saudi Arabia is often your employer (though not at Yorks) you will be reluctant to complain too much about housing inconveniences. If your landlord is a third party, he already has his rent and so disinterested in your problems. In my old office in Riyadh, several employees started complaining about the taste of the water. The building supervisor (actually, the owner's secretary) visited the building and after a quick walk-around announced that all was well.

But the unusual flavors continued to season the soup.

The employees complained again and management's response was that they were complainers and why were they spending so much time out of the office anyway? There was no problem with the water in the office. That is where they should be spending their time. But the complaints kept coming.

Finally, the owner was persuaded to hire a plumber who, being greatly experienced in these matters, went first to the cistern and found the remains of several dead cats. It was unclear why the howls of a drowning cat failed to keep other cats away. While the dead cats were removed, it would have been wasteful to dump all that water, especially given Riyadh's desert location. So the employees were told that the water was being recycled; and that was certainly true if you define "recyle" as "normal use."

On the bright side, only cats were found, and not rats or other animals. On the other hand, cats are not recreational swimmers and were probably in the area looking for food. Say, a rat, for instance. On the African veldt, all sorts of animals come to the oasis to drink. So it is unlikely that the cats were alone.

Don't Forget to Tape the Toilets

If you have the good fortune to be permanently based in Saudi Arabia you may find that you are entitled to home leave. A standard expat package usually provides for 45 days of leave. Yorks doesn't follow this practice, by the way. Aramco calls this "mandatory vacation" or "repat". During one such home leave, I packed my bag, turned off the lights and left my apartment in Suleimaniya. I needed to stay away longer than anticipated due to visa renewal problems. When these issues were resolved and I had my visa in hand, I returned to my apartment in Riyadh.

When I entered the apartment, something seemed—amiss. I imagined that the cleaning crew had been in and had not done a very good job. I lay on a bed which seemed excessively dusty. A window was open by a few millimeters in the dining room to permit a cable to enter but the dust storms are relentless. Still, I wasn't sure how the dust—if that was the source of the filth—had gotten into the bedroom. I decided, as I tried to settle myself to sleep, to take a sleeping pill, but having had bad experiences with Ambien I took something a little less overwhelming. I opened a small carton and pushed one lozenge through the tin foil. I left the package on the nightstand next to the bed and promptly fell asleep.

In the morning, I noticed that another lozenge had been

pushed through the foil and had broken apart in the center. The clear liquid had run out onto the nightstand. My first thought was that I had tried to get another lozenge out of the packaging and had broken it in the process. But I did not remember doing this. It seemed odd.

I went to the bathroom and saw a bar of soap in the tub. The soap appeared to have been gnawed. I then noticed tiny black pellets all over the place. I wondered why I hadn't seen them before. At first I thought they were dead insects, but that is before the rat ran past me into the bedroom. I shut the door after it. It was huge. Of course, that is what everyone says when they first find a rat in their apartment. The rat was locked behind the door and so, for the moment, could do no damage beyond what it was already responsible for. I looked at the toilet and saw that all of the water in the bowl had evaporated. The door to the apartment was locked. The pellets were everywhere. The bar of soap had been turned into a meal by the rat, who decided ultimately, that the fare did not meet his high standards.

Like most apartment dwellers facing a crisis of such magnitude, I decided that I would have to call the building's Super. Since I did not have a telephone in Suleimaniya–and if I did it is unlikely I would have known either his number or my own–I decided that the best thing to do would be to go to the office and call him from there. Leaving the rat locked in the bedroom, I left.

At the office, I explained my predicament and directed that the super be summoned to deal with the intruder. When I complained of the general state of filth and sanitation in the apartment, I was asked, "Did you tape the toilet?"

—Of course I didn't tape the toilet, I said. Why would anyone tape a toilet?

—So the rats don't come.

You might think, as you approach the bowl, that the water pooled there sits on top of a pillar of water stretching to the sewer system. This is not the case. The water sits in an S curve, unable to descend because of the curve of the drainage pipe. Below there is simply an empty pipe. Nothing more. When the water evaporates, there is nothing to prevent a rat from crawling up through the pipes and into the toilet. Not that the small amount of water in the bowl presents a serious obstacle; after all, rats can swim. For some reason, they rarely will swim up the bowl. But if the bowl is dry an intrepid rat may do so, only to be followed by other rats, each marking the walls of the pipe with pheromones from a gland underneath the tail like chalk marks made by Depression-era hoboes on a fence to tell the others that it is safe. Now there was a rat throughway into my bathroom. Rats are not solitary creatures. I only hoped that the rat in the bedroom was alone.

I spoke to the Super who expressed surprise at the presence of a rat in his building. He then asked me, —Did you tape the

toilet when you left? I confessed that I had not. "Well, what did

you expect?" he asked. I protested that no one had told me to tape the toilets, but as this falls into the category of information that one is expected to possess, my protests were summarily ignored. The Super promised me that he would send someone to examine the apartment immediately and get rid of the rat.

An hour later his assistant called to tell me he had been to my apartment and the rat was no longer there. —It probably left

the same way it came in, he said. I see that you didn't tape the toilet. I repeated that I had not, thanked him for his efforts, and

continued my working day. At the lunch break, I went home for a brief rest only to find that the door to the bedroom was still closed. The SuperâĂŹs assistant might have closed it after insuring that the rat was no longer there, but it was more likely that no one had visited the apartment at all. I opened the door; I didn't see the rat anywhere. To be sure, I started moving the furniture around to make sure that no rat was hiding. It was only when I opened the drapes that the rat ran out from under them and went underneath the bed.

I left the room and closed the door.

As the Super had failed in his mission I was next to despair. A rat had set up housekeeping in my apartment. More likely than not, the rat had leapt up onto the nightstand while I was sleeping, helped himself to a a sleeping lozenge and spat it out after finding it not to his liking. In the future, the rat would come and go as he pleased through the passageway of the toilet. Only God knows how many of his fellow rats would come to join him until there was nothing left to eat. For years I had taken friendly abuse from roommates, family and neighbors about my slovenliness. But now my reputation for slobbery had moved to the next level: my home had literally become a rat's nest. The rat had acquired squatter's rights and would not go easily. I returned to the office, worried about my next move.

I polled my colleagues at work about the problem. I hoped that someone knew of a precedent concerning rat eviction. Perhaps there was something in a real property text I had overlooked. An African colleague volunteered his expertise.

—Did you tape the toilet? he asked.
—No, I didn't know I was supposed to.

—You're lucky, my Sudanese friend said.

—How am I lucky? There's a rat living in my apartment.

—It's an Arab rat, he said. There's a difference. If it was an African rat, forget it. You'd never get rid of it.

—And why is that?

–There's no food in Africa. There's food here. African rats are tougher. A lot tougher. Catching this one will be easy.

He told me to go and buy a glue trap and some cat food.

—Put the cat food on the trap, open the door where the rat is hiding and go out to dinner. Stay away, maybe an hour. Maybe two. When you come back, the rat will be stuck on the trap.

And so it was. When I returned, there was the live rat, in the middle of my bedroom. Huge. This rat had to weigh at least three kilos. A glue trap does not kill a rat. There was no way that I could pick the rat up and throw it into the garbage, alive. It might become dislodged from the glue trap.

The only sure way, I thought, is to kill it.

Unfortunately, while everyone else in the country seemed to have access to any manner of weapons I did not. Nor did I possess an instrument suitable for a bludgeoning. A knife from the kitchen would be too messy, and besides, I did not want to sully a carving knife. I knew that no amount of cleaning or sterilization would rid the blade of the taint. I remembered that because of my skills at furniture assembly, a leg from a table bought at IKEA was wobbly. I unscrewed the table leg, took it in my hand, summoned up my furies and brought the IKEA table leg down on the rat's skull.

Only then could I throw the rat into the garbage. In the days that followed, the entire apartment was wiped with chlorine, following the same procedure used to clean a dwelling after a human body is found decaying inside.

I went to the bathroom and taped the toilet with silvery duct tape. Duct tape, sometimes called, "duck tape" is waterproof and strong. Years ago, a twenty-five year old man was kidnapped in Miami during a drug-deal gone bad. His head and face were wrapped in duct tape so as to asphyxiate him. At the murder trial, the jury saw the pictures of the deceased. One of them passed a note to the judge asking if the picture was accurate because the victim appeared to be in his 70's. Duct tape is powerful.

I now never forget to tape the toilets whenever I leave the Kingdom. That particular commode was never used again. It is permanently sealed with duct tape. I had no desire to meet any other revenge-seeking members of the pack while in a vulnerable position. I have not yet shared with IKEA the good news that in a pinch their furniture components might serve as weapons.

When most people look at the toilet they see a benign plumbing instrument, a necessary convenience because of our shared biology. Not me. When I look at a toilet, I see a portal to hell. Do not leave your apartment in Saudi Arabia for an extended period of time without taping the toilet. You have been warned.

Mail

In the 1940's, mail was still considered so new and literacy rates so low that the common practice in Riyadh was to take the arriving mail and dump it in the center of town—near Chop-Chop Square. If you were waiting for a letter you would go and see if it had arrived, and while there, if you saw a letter addressed to someone you knew you would pick it up and take it to them.

Things haven't changed much.

In many Saudi offices and apartment buildings you will find a stack of mail sitting on a counter waiting for—someone. Mail forwarding is unknown. Address correction is not practiced. Who will pay for the delivery of a misdirected letter? The post office denies blame and will not incur the costs of a new delivery. Ideally, the sender should pay, but there is no way to let him know. Return to Sender is not just the title of an Elvis Presley hit: it costs money. When the stack gets too high the older mail is thrown away leaving space for any new letters that might arrive until the pile gets too high again and the process is repeated. From time to time you might shuffle through the pile and if there is an envelope addressed to someone you know, you should feel free to take it and give it to him.

For the most part, street addresses are unknown. Reforms have been introduced to make the system usable. My old apartment building was assigned a number and new mailboxes were installed by the privatized Saudi postal service. Their eventual use is greatly anticipated. Unfortunately, no letters were ever delivered to the new mailboxes though someday they might be.

For this reason I tell people that there is no mail service in Saudi Arabia. This is not technically true but practically it is correct. The contradiction is that mail sent from Saudi Arabia will be accepted into the global mail delivery system and, barring unusual circumstances, will be delivered. Courier service into and out of Saudi Arabia is efficient though on the receiving end packages must go through Saudi customs where their contents may be rejected for unanticipated reasons: For example, PeptoBismol is banned for religious reasons because it contains bismuth, which is an element associated with hellfire and Satan (his Arabic name is *Iblis*). Stomach upset or not, importation is prohibited. Be careful what you eat.

Communications

Newspapers are routinely censored at the Ministry of Interior in Saudi Arabia before public sales are permitted. For this reason it is impossible to obtain the daily edition of any newspaper in the Kingdom. Each copy must be reviewed individually. If there is any content in the newspaper which offends the customs and traditions of the Kingdom of Saudi Arabia it is blacked out with a sharpie. The usual suspects are liquor or clothing advertisements which show too much skin. Usually other types of content—that is, words—are left alone, but not always. If the censors become aware that a particular article is controversial it will be deleted from the newspaper or magazine in question. This leaves the subscriber often wondering what exactly was published when the pages no longer run in sequence. A call to the newspaper or magazine will sometimes result in a copy of the offending article being sent by fax or email.

The ubiquity of the Internet in Saudi Arabia makes the manual elimination of advertising not only woefully anachronistic but a useless exercise. Still, print advertisements are different and perhaps it is the fear of their intrusion into the analog world that requires continued review by the Ministry of the Interior. Either that, or it is merely bureaucratic inertia.

Newspapers and magazines are not censored in Bahrain. *The*

Financial Times will come straight from the printer to the retailer to your greedy little mitts without any government intervention.

Though the censor can sometimes be avoided by turning to the Internet, the Internet itself is nevertheless censored in both Saudi Arabia and Bahrain. Prior to 2006 all Internet connections in the Kingdom went through a single proxy server and when it went down, so did your connection to the world. Technical innovations have superseded this method and the Kingdom now uses a DNS blacklist of prohibited sites. Bahrain uses a similar system to restrict access to officially objectionable sites. Pornography, alcohol and sites that criticize Islam are not surprisingly prohibited. As a result of this, the Internet in Saudi Arabia is safe for children.

Satellite television is widely available in the Kingdom. In theory this availability is on an experimental basis only. The experiment has been conducted for at least a decade and will probably be conducted for several decades more or at least until such time as satellite television, like the Betamax, beepers and other forms of old technology are overtaken by the new. Abandoned C band three meter dishes litter the roofs of many buildings. If you need your own dish, new one-meter dishes are sold in stores and technicians will install them cheerfully. That is, if they can find a rooftop place amongst the old rusting tech. Orbit Satellite(osnnetwork.com) is a good bet and has unfiltered broadband bi-directional Internet service as well. A wide variety of cable and premium channels are available. Expect to leave a SR 500 deposit for the decoder box and no, it is not necessary to have an *iqama* to purchase service.

Some compounds have their own satellite service provider and you can hook up in the same way that you would connect to cable television services in North America. If you are hooked on

MuchMusic there is no reason to go cold turkey merely because you live in Saudi Arabia.

Unlike some countries in the Gulf, neither Saudi Arabia nor Bahrain restricts VoIP service. This means that Skype, Vonage, MagicJack and their competitors will work without any problems other than excessive latency if you use a bidirectional satellite connection. It is best to configure your VoIP system before leaving North America. On arrival, you can plug the device in and you will have the same local number you had back home and when your friends call you, for them it will be a local call. Unfortunately, nothing can be done about the time difference. Just a few years ago monthly telephone bills in the hundreds of dollars were commonplace amongst expats trying to handle personal business or stay in touch with their families. This is no longer the case.. With the money you save you will have enough for an extra trip. If only you could take it.

Khobar Attacks

In 2004 the Jerusalem Squadron of Al Qaeda in the Arabian Peninsula launched a series of coordinated attacks on targets in the Eastern Province. One of the principal targets was the Oasis compound. It was a strange attack because despite the best efforts of Saudi law enforcement, many of the assailants escaped with their weapons in station wagons. There were two lesser-known targets of the attack: the Petroleum Building and the Remote Office Building.

It is for that reason that security in and around our offices is tight. The doors are electronically controlled and are manufactured with reinforced glass. The outer doors are bulletproof. Still, it is unlikely that Al Qaeda would be interested in repeating the attack–there is an armed personnel carrier mounted with a .50 caliber machine gun stationed at the front door. If the machine gun is insufficient disincentive, the location of the building in a construction zone should be: in the context of urban guerrilla warfare, it is a great defense.

Sadly, during the attack a young boy was killed in a compound nearby. It is said that he wanders the building at night, looking for his father. Some have heard noises; papers are mysteriously moved or machines turned off or on for no apparent reason. *Djinns*, creatures of Islamic cosmology, usually cannot be bothered to engage in such misbehavior. They do not want us mistaking them for mere poltergeists. Fear started to take hold amongst some of those who worked after hours. Once the guards have gone, the electric locks are set and getting out of the building can be challenging. Being locked inside a building with a wandering, lonely and probably hungry spirit is a challenge that few consulting firms have to face. Fortunately, at Yorks we know how to deal with all types of problems, whether of this world or the next.

Because spirits are often hungry we placed a bowl of rice in an inconspicuous corner of the storage room so that the spirit of the young boy would find something to eat. Additionally, we left a toy football so he would have something to play with and hopefully leave us alone.

Apparently these offerings have been accepted for the incidence of the inexplicable has dropped significantly. If you come across the offerings in the storage room, please leave them there. Children can react violently when toys are taken away from them.

Reading List

New consultants are usually told to familiarize themselves with local regulations when arriving in a a new jurisdiction. Unfortunately there is no single text that I can suggest to help the newly recruited consultant get up to speed. So, this reading list is designed to provide a place to start. *The History of Saudi Arabia*, by Aleixi Vassiliev provides historical context. Vassiliev, a former Pravda correspondent, wrote a comprehensive history of Saudi Arabia. My copy was lent to a colleague at some point during my career and never returned.

Familiarization with the Qu'ran is important. Saudi Arabia's Basic Law states that the Qu'ran and the *sunnah* (traditions) of the Prophet are the country's source of law. This provides for some interesting distinctions even in otherwise routine commercial law. Honoring contractual obligations is not merely a civil obligation but a solemn religious mandate.

The *hadith* are the reports of the sayings and practices of the Prophet. These really are for specialists and can be safely ignored at this stage in your training. One compiler, Bukhari, found 3000 of these traditions to be authentic. Unfortunately, he found another 297,000 which he deemed to be unreliable or manufactured. They are rarely cited in the documents that will comprise your workload. You will see Qu'ranic authority mentioned from time to time, and contracts often contain prayerful dedications. Professor Frank Vogel is a Saudi legal expert and has been so qualified by several U.S. Federal district courts. Anything he has written on the subject of the Kingdom will be useful.

Other than Saudi Aramco's illicit but highly sought-after pamphlet titled *The Blue Flame*, there are few underground or samizdat publications that purport to describe the Saudi experience. Jean Sasson has written a series of books about Saudi royals. Her *Princess* is widely known and gives a look inside one branch of the Royal family. *Paramedic to the Prince* by Patrick Notestine is a must-read account about life at the top and the Saudi healthcare establishment. *Tales of the Unexpected in the Magic Kingdom* by Farqhurat Phlegmton is an irreverent look at life in the Kingdom. The Saudi government tried to ban the broadcast years ago of the BBC's *Death of a Princess*, so there must have been something in it that bothered them greatly. Certainly the film will not be playing at the local cinema in Riyadh. Oh wait, there are no cinemas in Riyadh.

You can also start reading the *Arab News*, or as much of it as they let on line. The front few pages of the newspaper are printed on green paper, hence its local nickname, *The Green Truth*. The on line experience is less than satisfactory. "This content is only found in the print edition" is a frequent warning on the website. In reading the *Arab News*, be careful not to skim the headlines as often there will be an "in other news" break in the middle of the article which has nothing to do with the rest of the story. For example, an article about a ribbon-cutting at some newly built facility may contain a report about the status of the long-anticipated new Mortgage Law. Or the long-anticipated new Companies Law. Or something else that is equally long-awaited.

Another useful source for learning about the Kingdom is the blogosphere. *Religious Policeman* was an entertaining and informative blog that is no longer being maintained. Still, as Ezra Pound said, "literature is news that stays news" and many of the observations and commentary there remain valid long after their sell-by date.

Bahrain

Bahrain is Tijuana. It's not of course, but this is how Saudi Arabia looks at it: an amusement park filled with alcohol and a place for misbehavior. Before the King Fahad Causeway was built linking what are now the two Kingdoms travel was difficult and not really a weekend proposition. Saudis know that not all women are veiled in Bahrain, alcohol is plentiful and the rules they faithfully live by are not enforced. For the average Saudi, Bahrain is a playground and unless you are playing there is no good reason to go there. Warnings against STD's are sometimes handed out in Arabic at the border.

Bahrain today is a kingdom with a king, but until 2002, like Qatar, Bahrain was merely a "state". Both Bahrain and Saudi Arabia are member states of the Gulf Cooperation Council. Citizens of one member state do not need passports to travel to another. You would think this would speed transits between the two countries but it does not.

It is extremely difficult to convince a Saudi that any work is done in Bahrain at all. Saudis do not believe that anyone really works in Bahrain and will view such a claim with deep suspicion. They know what they like to do in the little Kingdom and assume that is what everyone else comes for as well. For Saudis, Bahrain is merely a fiesta, an outlet for desires difficult to satisfy on the green side of the Causeway.

If this is the Bahrain you are looking for you will have no trouble finding it. There is a large sin industry serving Saudi guests and visitors, most of whom arrive on Thursday after work, and go back on Saturday afternoon. Bahrain has a healthy appetite for and tolerance of sin. Forbidden pork sandwiches are available at some restaurants. A hamburger at McDonald's in Bahrain is called a hamburger while the same sandwich in Saudi is called a "beefburger" to avoid even the suggestion of pork. The only real surprise is that, given the Arab world's love of gambling, there is no casino, not even a clandestine one– or at least, not one that I have been able to find. There is no high-stakes card room, either. There is a business opportunity here.

Freedom in Bahrain extends to religious belief. There are many churches and even a synagogue. Russian Orthodox Christmas is celebrated–primarily by Desi Bahrain–according to the Julian calendar.

Prior to the beginning of the Arab Spring, Bahrain was a growing banking and corporate center in competition with Dubai. Political unrest caused many companies to fold their tents and leave. Having survived the economic downturn in 2008, it is a shame that Bahrain is having difficulty surviving the political upheavals of 2011. At the time of this writing (May, 2012) it is unclear when things will get back to normal. The exodus of business continues and recently a Japanese bank announced its relocation to Dubai. The individuals protesting the government and the lack of jobs have frightened many of those jobs away. They may never come back.

Apart from the debauched Saudi Bahrain, there are other Bahrains. There is a family Bahrain where a husband and wife can watch a movie together, hear live music, visit a pub or have dinner in a public place. There is a Desi Bahrain which has its back turned on Saudi Arabia and turns towards India. There is a British expat Bahrain, centered at the British Club and the Rugby club. These Bahrains have little to do with Saudi Arabia. For the most part, though they occupy the same physical space as the other Bahrains, they rarely mix.

In his book *Arabia* Jonathan Raban wrote,

"What appeared to be unique to Bahrain was the way in which so many nationalities had landed upon one small patch of ground, coming together to create not a cosmopolitan city but a multitude of tiny provincial hamlets. Few expatriates ever bothered to learn more than a word or two of Arabic; they had no Arab friends; they were comfortably ignorant of the lives of the people with whom they shared this meager acreage of land. The same was true, apparently, of the Arabs themselves, the Iranians, the Indians, the Pakistanis. The different groups exchanged contracts, employed one another, purchased things at each other shops, were each other's landlords and tenants- -but they didn't mix."

This is still true today.

Women come to Bahrain from Saudi Arabia for a taste of freedom. Saudi women need not wear their *abayas*. Saudi women who have obtained European or North American driver's licenses can rent cars and drive on Bahraini streets to their heart's content. A woman can go on a date without worrying that a man with a stick may come to beat her. Public displays of affection are disfavored in Bahrain as well as Saudi, but it is not uncommon to see couples holding hands at malls in Manama. Men may be seen holding hands as well, but this Arab custom has little to do with romantic affection.

Because up until recently obtaining visas to Bahrain was so easy, there is also a tourist Bahrain. European tourists, albeit in relatively small numbers, come in the winter to get away from the cold, or perhaps to explore another place once they have tired of Dubai. There remains a special relationship with the United Kingdom whose passport holders are normally entitled to a no-fee visa, though things can change at any time.

At Yorks, unless you are Canadian, it is unlikely that you will be assigned to Bahrain. The Bahrain you will see will be the weekend Bahrain. Be careful about drawing conclusions from this limited view. Living in Bahrain is different. There are many cultural and educational opportunities that are simply unavailable in the Kingdom.

For this reason, Saudi workers who have the choice will usually work in Bahrain if they can tolerate the commute.

Language

Arabic is the national language of Saudi Arabia. It is the predominant language of the Arabian Peninsula, which the Romans called *Arabia Felix*. It is a Semitic language which was fixed in writing in the 7th century AD at a time when English was Saxon and had not suffered the influence of Romance languages which only occurred four centuries later with the Norman Conquest.

A person who can read Arabic can pick up the Koran and read the 7th century text. Can you say the same of Beowulf?

Despite this venerable tradition, you may find the ubiquity of English surprising in the Kingdom. English is the language of commerce and to a surprising extent of everyday life. A Saudi needing to order a bucket of chicken for his family at KFC will do so in English, as the chances that the workers will be fluent in Arabic are slim. You may also see a family's driver hand a mobile phone over the counter to give counter staff an order. While this behavior is appropriate in Saudi fast food restaurants, sending your driver with a mobile phone is not an accepted way to attend a meeting. From time to time this does happen. Once you become accustomed to sending your driver out for chicken sending him to a board meeting might seem a logical next step.

But English is found not only at fast food restaurants. Contract work will be conducted primarily in English. Documents will be marked up and exchanged in English. Discussions about the various drafts will similarly be held in English. When the negotiations are completed, an Arabic translation will be made. Sometimes it is easy to tell from the translation that the document started out in English. This is true even of some Saudi government agencies. In fact, sometimes Saudi government agencies conduct their meetings in English. While this is not universally the case, do not be surprised if you come across the practice. Sometimes meetings will spontaneously switch from one language to the other, even at the highest levels.

If you make the decision that you want to learn the language, finding Arabic classes in Riyadh is no easy task. There is a Berlitz office, but if you find the Berlitz method tedious because you are left to your own devices to figure out the grammar, there are few alternatives.Classes in Quranic Arabic are offered, but these are more concerned with religious orthodoxy than ordering take-out chicken (the key Arab phrase for take-out chicken is *capsa safarin*). Complicating the problem is that most textbooks or teaching systems–and even the Rosetta Stone program–insist on teaching the Arabic writing system before you learn much of the language. This is no trivial task. As a start, there are 24 consonants in Arabic and each has three forms. This means 72 glyphs must be learned. Vowels are sometimes written and sometimes they are not. Add to these diacritical marks, ligatures and the unfamiliarity of writing from right to left and, as most expats have done, you may give up.

This is unfortunate because Arab teenagers on their own perfected a perfectly functional system for writing Arabic, called *arabizi*. The system uses the Roman alphabet and the numbers 3, 5, 7 and 9 for those sounds which are exclusive to Arabic. The beauty of the system is that you can sound out a word and write it without having to learn the Arabic writing system and anyone can read it. At least, anyone with a mobile phone, because *arabizi* was created to make it easier to send SMS messages, and in the process a standardized writing system was created. Why this is not widely adopted in the West for the teaching of Arabic is beyond me.

Think that you at least know the numbers? You don't. They are called Arabic numerals, but the Arabic version is only somewhat familiar. It is very useful to learn how to read numbers in Arabic. Even though the language is written right to left, the numbers are read from left to right, from high to low in value. Most seem familiar but that seven is actually a six and what looks like an obese zero is really the number five. Two helpful tricks: the number "seven opens to heaven". The phrase will help you remember the difference between seven and eight. To distinguish between two and three, note that the three has a small three resting on the top of the stalk. That should help you remember the difference. You already know 0, 1 and 9.

What about pronunciation? Here's a hack: pronounce Arabic like Spanish. Yes, this is incorrect and your accent will sound a bit funny (alright, a lot funny) to a native speaker. But 90% of the time you will be close enough to be understood. If you do not know how to pronounce Spanish, then you might as well try to learn the Arabic pronunciation. Otherwise, your high school Spanish can be dusted off in a pinch.

The word "*abu*" means, "father of." The familiar way to address a Saudi is not by his first name, but the word "*abu*" followed by the name of his firstborn son. This can get confusing if Abu Hussam and Hussam are in the same room together. If a man does not have a son, you use "*abu*" and the name of his eldest daughter. Thus, if your wife, or one of your wives, gives birth to a boy when all of your children were girls you will find that your own name has changed in middle age. My godfather had six daughters before his first son; I do not believe Uncle Vince would have felt comfortable changing his name so late in life. This is sometimes the first clue for a young girl of the different treatment Saudi society accords men and women.

The familiar way to address a woman is to use the term "*umm*", or "mother of." But be careful: "*Umm Ali*" might refer to Ali's mother or a popular Saudi dessert, known for its supposed aphrodisiacal qualities.

During most of Islamic history, most Muslims did not have last names. Kemal Mustafa, known as Ataturk, insisted that Turks take last names as part of his modernization of Turkey.

In the Gulf, a surname is followed by a tribal name. There are eighteen or so major tribes in Saudi Arabia, and according to the tribes, some are incompatible with others. These traditions and rivalries predate Islam. In a recent notorious case, a Saudi judge granted a divorce at the request of a woman's family due to tribal incompatibility even though neither husband nor wife had asked for a divorce. There was both a domestic as well as an international outcry since such grounds for divorce are not recognized in Islam.

The common way of addressing people is by using the English honorific "Mister" in front of a man's first name, and the word "Madame" in front of a woman's. Do not be surprised if you are addressed as Mister. Sam, and if your name is Sue, Madame Sue.

The word "*al*" in Arabic is the definite article and is not short for Alexander. I made this mistake early in my career, trying to find someone named Al at the Al Jeraisy establishment in Riyadh. I assumed that he was the founder of the business and was quite embarrassed by my error. a mistake often made by new arrivals. I hope that by telling you this I have kept you from making the same mistake.

Police

There are five different institutions through which the Saudi state exercises power. Four have analogs in the West, the fifth does not. The first is the Army. Next is the red beret-wearing National Guard, an elite force which has the obligation of protecting the Royal Family.

Third is the police. In addition to performing a function similar to the police in the West, Saudi police are much more involved in the lives of everyday people. It is not uncommon for exasperated parents to deliver an unruly teenager to the police because he is talking back to them. After a day or two in jail and a general talking-to, the youngster is usually returned to his family with orders to behave and an open invitation to return in case the bad behavior is repeated.

Faced with an unusual event the police may simply decide to arrest everyone on the simple basis that something screwy is going on and that the matter needs to be sorted out. If it takes a while to get things sorted, so be it. Civil debts can be a basis for incarceration as well: make your credit card payments timely. A confessed debtor can be held in jail until he pays up. Some have languished for years, trying to convince the police and their creditors that they have no funds to pay.

The fourth, the secret police, are known as the *mubahith*.

They are the most feared. Their powers are derived directly from the King and they are responsible to him alone. They are the ones who will take you away in the middle of the night and hold you incommunicado at the pleasure of the King. The Saudi Rules of Criminal Procedure do not apply to those so held. There is a law authorizing detention but what happens to those detained is explained only in the body of another law which is itself classified. Targeted are those who are perceived as existential threats to the Saudi state, those who might drum up popular support and those whose crimes are political in nature. Political dissidents may be held for years unless and until they decide to behave or they become too old and leave their fight for another generation. You can expect *mubahith* officers to be Western-trained—at places like the University of Arizona—and to speak perfect, unaccented English.

The fifth institution has no analog in the West: the Religious Police, or the Commission for the Promotion of Virtue and the Prevention of Vice, popularly called the *muttawa*. The *muttawa* consists of a trained, 4000 man force. They are spotted easily. Most Saudi men wear native dress called a *thobe*, a cassock-like garment which except in winter is almost always white and which runs almost to the floor. The *muttawa* wear distinctive short thobes which stop just above the ankles in case it becomes necessary to run while fighting for the Faith. *Muttawa* always have long beards. Some carry long sticks which they use to threaten or beat those who do not obey them. They never patrol by themselves but are accompanied by another *muttawa* or increasingly, a police officer. Today they are supposed to wear identifying name tags in Arabic.

The use of police officers to accompany the *muttawa* on their rounds is a fairly recent innovation. It used to be unclear as to whether *muttawa* had arrest powers. With or without these powers they often made arrests. The government decided that they should not have arrest powers and so now they are accompanied by a policeman in case arrests are necessary.

Despite the new rules, *muttawa* sometimes continue to make arrests because they feel they answer only to a higher authority. In recent years the *muttawa* have been criticized for being out of control so the government clarified the rules in order to reign them in. Police officers accompany the *muttawa* to chaperone them and curb their excesses.

They are not always successful. The worst excess happened in Riyadh in 2002. A fire started in a girl's high school and the *muttawa* blocked the exits because the girls were trying to escape without wearing their *abayas*. The *muttawa* forced the girls back into the burning school where at least fifteen died. This caused an internal uproar and the protests against the *muttawa* were heard internationally. After that, the government began to slowly circumscribe their powers. Nevertheless, you will see them in shopping malls making sure that shops close for prayer and exhorting people who "appear" to be Muslims to pray. They may question couples who look suspicious (whatever this means) and demand documentation of their status. Recently a Youtube video of *muttawa* accosting a young woman for wearing nail polish went viral.

In addition to such community service, the *muttawa* also conduct stings trying to catch sorcerers, fortune tellers and booze merchants. These stings are operated much like narcotic buy-busts conducted by law enforcement in the West and have just as little effect. Mauretanian witches seem to be of particular interest to the *muttawa*. Moroccan women have been targeted because of a popular Saudi belief that they are able to bewitch husbands.

Presumably, the Saudi husbands have more than a little to do with the efficacy of Moroccan charms. These supernatural arrests and general goings-on are regularly reported in the *Arab News*.

Like other Saudis, *muttawa* have been exposed to Hollywood movies and in addition to their undercover work have been responsible for spectacular car chases around the country. The new President of the Commission, Abdullatif Aal Al-Sheikh, has recently reassured the public that the car chases will stop. Unfortunately, they have not. The undercover patrols, however, will be reduced. Sheikh Abdullatif has pointed out that the *muttawa's* function is to "correct the behavior of the young and old alike" but has acknowledged that the *muttawa* have committed mistakes. In defense of the institution, he claims that often the *muttawa* have been provoked. When it comes to questioning women about their prayer habits, the Sheikh said that his forces should instead "leave these matters to Almighty Allah who knows the secrets and ins and outs of His slaves."

On a daily basis you are most likely to run into the *muttawa* and the police. With respect to the *muttawa*, do not travel or be in the company of an unrelated woman, at least in Riyadh. To do so is to court trouble. This is less of a problem in Khobar but even the Eastern Province is becoming more conservative than it was ten years ago.

You are most likely to have interactions with the police at checkpoints. Usually Westerners are waived through because as a general rule the police officers manning the checkpoints are not fluent in English. Unless, of course, they are part of a *mubahith* operation and are looking for a Westerner.

They might be looking for you.

Gender

I hesitate to write anything about gender, though in Saudi Arabia the very strangeness and great differences in the way society treats women is of immense interest to the rest of the world. To give you some idea of the complexity of the relationship between men and women in Saudi Arabia, King Abdulazziz frequently referred to himself as "the brother of Noor," the name of his eldest sister. While Saudi women legally have little power, in Islam they are equal and at home they rule.

Islamic family law is highly complex and contains many specific and idiosyncratic rules. Some of these are quite modern– in the 8th century a woman could inherit and hold property in her own name and dispose of her funds herself without interference by her husband or relatives. Legally, in Saudi Arabia women are treated as minors are in Western countries. Because of this limited legal status they must obtain the permission or assistance of their guardian before engaging in business or carrying out civil activities.

If you are invited to a traditional Saudi home you will see that entertaining is segregated. Men socialize together and women, except for servants, are rarely seen.

Eve-teasers

In their never ending mission to segregate the sexes, the religious police have convinced shopping mall owners not to permit young, unmarried men into the malls in the evening. There is no relevant Saudi law on the subject besides the institutional preference of the *muttawa* to keep men and women apart as much as possible. In their defense, the *muttawa* claim that the young men harass the women. This harassment amounts to efforts to obtain telephone numbers. Keep in mind that it is a daunting task to obtain a telephone number from a fully-veiled woman. Nevertheless, life finds a way. Bluetooth is one way (you can have your smart phone discover nearby devices) and numbers can be passed back and forth in this fashion. Some young men paint their Blackberry Messenger number on their car or truck in the hopes that someone will give them a call.

One meme–allegedly based on a true story–involved a young man who kept pestering a veiled woman for her phone number. He would not give up. Finally, she lifted her veil to show that she not only already knew the young man, but was his mother. This anecdote has even made it to the screen in a Saudi television comedy, *Tash ma Tash*, which very unfortunately does not have a subtitled version.

Young Saudi women, like young women everywhere, are hardly blameless in this endless game of cat and mouse. One year there was even a scandal over "indecent" *abayas*. These were embroidered with barely discernible phrases like, "Dare you touch me?" in black velvet on a black background. The *muttawa* successfully prohibited the importation of such *abayas*. However, since many *abaya* are custom madeskilled seamstresses can provide any legend the customer fancies.

In the Kingdom it is often one step forward, two steps back. During the past few months, a policy change was announced so as to permit mall owners to allow single men to enter the malls in the evening. This was after many families protested that there was nothing for their sons to do in the Kingdom.

When a shopping mall is your sole source of entertainment, there can be unanticipated consequences. Several people were trampled to death at the opening of the IKEA furniture store in Jeddah. Even though Sheikh Al-Sheikh has announced a kinder, gentler *muttawa*, the new shopping mall policy was quickly followed up with a government edict from the Office of the Prince in charge of Riyadh who advised that there would be an increase in enforcement to stop the Eve-teasing, which is the term the *Arab News* uses to describe these shopping mall shenanigans

Women and Driving

It is well known that women are not permitted to drive in Saudi Arabia. The ostensible reason is to keep men and women apart, for in Islam, "when a man and a woman are alone together, the Devil accompanies them." But this rule apparently only applies to some men. Women are not forbidden from riding in automobiles, but they must have a driver. So some women sit all day in the car with their drivers being driven from pillar to post. The drivers are never Saudi, but come from countries like the Sudan, the Philippines or Pakistan. It is somewhat silly to think that because Saudi rules say these men "don't count" that human nature can be avoided or ignored. Relationships between women and their drivers do occur. Such a relationship is viewed as scandalous by society and the woman is always ostracized by her family and the driver deported.

Saudi sex segregation rules ignore store employees as well. Finding a female shop attendant is difficult and the rules forbidding women working in shops have recently been relaxed so as to permit female shop attendants in stores selling intimate wear. The fact that previously only foreign men worked in these shops was ignored because the non-Saudi male workers were simply not taken into account. So the rules segregating the sexes are designed to deter the mixing of male and female Saudis but often fail to take into account non-Saudi males.

Marriage

If you meet the love of your life, do not expect to be able to get married in Saudi Arabia unless you are a Muslim. Even if you are a Muslim, there are a few serious administrative obstacles. First, the religious: a Muslim male may marry a Muslim, Christian or Jewish female, but Christian or Jewish males may not marry a Muslim female. A Muslim male may not marry a Buddhist or a Hindu as these faiths are considered polytheistic and forbidden. A Saudi needs permission from the civil authorities to marry a foreigner in Saudi Arabia. If permission is not obtained, the marriage will not be recognized and the spouse not given a visa. However, nothing stops Saudis from traveling outside the Kingdom and marrying in accordance with the laws of another country.

In theory, a Christian man should be able to marry a Christian woman in Saudi Arabia but I have never heard of a Saudi wedding license being granted under these circumstances. I have heard of non-Saudi Muslim men taking advantage of the Islamic rules concerning polygamy to take a second or third (or even fourth) wife when doing so is forbidden in their own countries. Though Tunisia is a Muslim country, as one Tunisian told me, *c'est interdit* which means, "forget it."

In the Eastern Province and Bahrain you may come across the phenomenon of *misyar*, or temporary marriage. This is a shi'a religious concept allowing for time-limited marriages. In order to discourage adultery, the shi'a normalize more casual relationships in the eyes of God through a marriage with an expiration date. I have not heard of a non-Muslim taking advantage of the concept and for orthodox Sunni Muslims, entering into such marriages is forbidden. This is why most Saudi men have a keen interest in the subject. If you hear about "sushi" marriages this has nothing to do with a couple sharing a fondness for Japanese cuisine but instead refers to a type of mixed marriage, that is, between Sunni and Shi'a.

Despite these theological innovations, in Saudi Arabia an unmarried couple cannot live together legally. In Bahrain, no one cares. This is why the Yorks prohibition on living in Bahrain and working in Saudi Arabia is more significant than one might otherwise realize.

After you have been in Saudi for a while, surreal song lyrics such as Bob Dylan's, "The second mother was with the seventh son/And they were both out on Highway 61" will seem unremarkable. In Saudi Arabia, the surreal is commonplace.

Mixed Dining

In Riyadh, the only place where men and women can dine in public is in one of the restaurants at the Al Khozama hotel on Olaya Street. It may be that newer hotels on Olaya Street, such as the Four Seasons in Kingdom Center, also permit the practice. Otherwise it is forbidden. At Kingdom Mall, in the complex adjacent to the hotel, mixed dining is definitely not permitted. At the Hard Rock restaurant there have been some horrible scenes involving the religious police and foreign businessmen and women. The only safe place is at the Al Khozama, which was once the only hotel in the area and for some reason foreigners are left alone.

In Khobar, you can have business meetings with women you are not married to at the Fusion restaurant on the second floor of the Royal Meridian Hotel as well as the main restaurant and cafe at the Mövenpick.

Diversity

Racism is alive and well in the Kingdom of Saudi Arabia and manifests itself even in official ways. For example, it is common for a company to have different salary scales based on the nationalities of its workers. An Egyptian accountant performing the same work as a Canadian accountant will be paid less. In both cases, compared to salaries in the worker's home country, the amounts paid are generous. But when co-workers of different nationalities compare pay stubs there will be friction. The concept of equal pay for equal work is unknown in the Kingdom.

Another issue is the classification of workers who come from countries that are diverse or which celebrate diversity. How do you classify a Canadian accountant who happens to be of Pakistani descent? And whose name is clearly Pakistani? Since much of Saudi Arabia's manual labor comes from the subcontinent, the treatment of these workers is often less than exemplary. This is why in labor disputes you often see individuals making a point of the fact that they hold a Canadian or European passport though their historic roots lie elsewhere. During the Lebanese War of 2006, the Canadian Embassy in Riyadh was surprised by the number of Canadian passport holders who came to seek aid. Many of these new Canadians also held Lebanese passports and in Saudi Arabia, are treated as Lebanese—and assigned to the

Levantine pay scale—despite their knowledge of the Canadian national anthem. In Saudi Arabia, having two or three passports makes little difference.

A recognized danger of institutionalized racism is the imposition of stereotypes. Often this starts in a benign fashion: Egyptian Coptic Christians are sought-after receptionists because they are native speakers of Arabic and do not take breaks for prayer. Is this cynicism or taking advantage of a fact? True Arabic-English bilingualism is institutionalized in the Sudan and the law curriculum follows that in the U.K. The university in Khartoum produces fully bilingual lawyers who hold professional degrees, so hiring a Sudanese lawyer can be a smart move.

Unfortunately, discarded and repulsive racial and ethnic stereotypes are heard all too often in Saudi Arabia, so do not be surprised when you hear them. How to react? The best way is not to ignore the slight but to gently and politely voice your disagreement. Saudis live in two worlds and when speaking English they inhabit ours. They know that these beliefs are improper and that we reject this bigotry. To say nothing is to tacitly approve and so join as an accomplice.

Homosexuality is illegal in Saudi Arabia and the punishment is death. Despite this oppressive legal environment, many gay men say that Saudi Arabia is paradise on earth. Go figure.

Alcohol

The Qu'ran did not contain an absolute prohibition on alcohol in the *ayas* (verses) of early revelation. It was only after the Prophet Mohammad saw the Faithful showing up for prayers while intoxicated that a final *aya* was revealed which contained the general prohibition.

Today, the importation of alcohol in any quantity is illegal. This rule is unlikely to change. Because alcohol is prohibited in Saudi Arabia, it is even more popular than in places where it is permitted. Some believe that alcohol was always prohibited in the Kingdom, but that is not true. Until the late 1950's, alcohol was openly sold and obtainable in the Kingdom. Saudi Aramco even operated liquor stores. Things changed after a party at the British consulate in Jeddah where a Saudi prince shot and killed a British diplomat. King Abdulazziz took a dim view of the matter and then banned alcohol generally. When the general prohibition on alcohol came into force, AramcoâĂŹs Chemistry Division was tasked with putting together a guide for the home distiller. Twenty years later, the official origins of the pamphlet, called *The Blue Flame* had been forgotten and the company tried to seize whatever copies it could find. Years later, Saudi Arabia is one of the biggest illegal importers of Johnny Walker Black.

Local laws prohibiting alcohol are not enforced within foreign embassies. In Riyadh there is an embassy circuit with different embassies holding parties or functions on a rotating basis. It is possible to construct a social life just by attending all of these different functions. If you are lucky enough to be invited to an embassy party you can drink as much as you want. Of course, if you take this literally and misbehave, you probably will not be invited back. Some countriesâĂŹ embassies are more stingy than others when it comes to the provision of booze to their citizens and guests. Others sell drink tickets at their parties to discourage excessive drinking. It is difficult for embassies to bring alcohol into the country in quantity. Those countries that have access to regular military flights have a higher level of generosity. The American Embassy, for example, boasts a full bar, called "Uncle Sam's." The British Embassy has no such facility. The Canadian Embassy has a discreet bar which, as far as I know, does not have a name. Getting an invite to these bars is not that easy because these establishments are primarily for embassy personnel. While alcohol is not incompatible with the social aspects of a country's basic mission, an embassy's prime function is not, rumors to the contrary, to be a booze oasis.

Embassies usually go all-out for their national day and sometimes an invitation can be had merely by asking for one. In the Eastern Province, there are U.S. and British consulates in Jeddah and Dhahran where alcohol-friendly events are had from time to time. The U.S. consulate in Dhahran has an active social scene and sometimes holds parties; if you register with them you increase your chances of an invitation. One does not have to be an American citizen to attend the functions. In recent years the social scene at the Consulate has diminished somewhat because of the attraction of Bahrain. It is much easier to simply cross the Causeway if you are suffering the need for a drink.

In addition to parties thrown by the various embassies, some embassy staff have a lucrative sideline selling booze that they have smuggled in. At one embassy, a junior diplomat realized that with his diplomatic plates and immunity he had an opportunity to really start paying down the mortgage back home. He started driving to Bahrain on the weekends and driving right back with a trunk full of Johnny Black, which sells for SR 800 a bottle. Soon he was making an additional $2500 or so per week. Everyone in the embassy knew what was going on and the ambassador of the country involved tried to rotate him back to his home country. The junior diplomat claimed that this would constitute a hardship because his children were in school, so they let him stay until the end of the school term. His customers were relieved. The problem with a sales channel like this is that while it lasts things are great, but diplomats rarely spend more than two years in the Kingdom and the business is not always bequeathed to a newly arriving colleague.

If you have no access to an embassy you are not necessarily out of luck. In several of the compounds you may find reasonable facsimiles of British pubs. Places like the Celtic Club, Tudor Rose and the Empire Club once operated openly. According to the Saudi authorities, the business was so lucrative that one of the owners was murdered in a business dispute. The British government maintained that this was nonsense and that Al Qaeda or others were to blame. In any event, the case called the "British Bombers" had the attention of the world media after a string of bombings which started in December, 2000 and continued until 2002.

The BAE compound has a friendly pub, but in this pub the booze on offer is usually of the local variety. For beer, this means serving non-alcoholic beer to which alcohol has been added, though some people brew beer from scratch. For wine, it means serving a potion which started out as grape juice from Austria.

The local distilled spirit is called *sid* which is short for *siddiqui* (loyal, trustworthy). It is also a title bestowed on the trustworthy, but *sid* is anything but. It tastes like strong mouthwash and there is no way to know in advance how strong it will be. If you do not like the local swill Johnny Black is available; the current price is around SAR 800 per bottle. Case discounts are usually not given. The trade is enormously lucrative.

Some of the supplies needed for booze-making can be obtained in the Kingdom. Others, like Bentonite, need to be acquired elsewhere. This can sometimes create additional problems. No one—that is, no one outside of Saudi Arabia—is going to get too excited about shipping packets of yeast by mail. Unfortunately, Bentonite is a white powder and shipping white powder by mail attracts all sorts of unwelcome attention. Vats used for fermentation used to be a problem, but the proliferation of five gallon plastic water jugs has provided a solution. You will still need a one-way valve. If you do not kill the fermentation process completely and use empty screw-cap Perrier bottles to bottle your vintage, you may get secondary fermentation in the bottle which converts the wine to champagne.

If all of this running around and second-rate science lesson is too much for you, you can always drive across the Causeway to Bahrain. There you will find two or three package stores. Otherwise, in Bahrain alcohol is permitted only in hotels and a few grandfathered places like the British Club, RickâĂŹs American Restaurant and some restaurants in Adliya.

Probably the most important advice concerning alcohol for the new employee is that if you think you have a drinking problem, seek help before you come to the Kingdom. Your problem will only get worse. There are AA chapters in the alcohol-free Kingdom. In the Eastern Province, one is on the Saudi Aramco compound but no ID is required to be shown to attend. Meetings are held in Building 1190 which is adjacent to medical facilities. More information can be found at http://aa-saudiarabia.me/. There is another meeting in Al Khobar.

Desire for the good stuff can even overwhelm the most faithful. There was once a *muttawa* who came to an office to check if staff were given sufficient time to go to the mosque to pray. The fact that the *muttawa* could not pray himself while he attempted to herd others to the mosque was not addressed. The *muttawa* in question had visited the office of the manager in order to administer a dressing-down. The manager apologized for his lack of hospitality–it was Ramadan and he could not offer tea. Reaching into his desk drawer, he told the *muttawa* that there was something else he could offer him.

–Would you like the red or the black? –The red or the black? Close the door! I don't want anyone to see!

The manager got up, walked over to his office door and closed it. He then returned to his desk and removed two illustrated company calendars, one red and one black.

The *muttawa* was crestfallen.

–That's it? Don't you have anything else? The manager explained that his brother ran a hotel in a neighboring country.

–I'll go tomorrow, the *muttawa* said.

And so he did. The report from the brother is that the *muttawa* had a bottle of the black brought to his room, which he finished in one evening.

There is a good word which comprehensively describes this human failing: hypocrisy.

Religion

Prayer Times

In Saudi Arabia you must familiarize yourself with the concept of prayer times, or *salat*. Sunni Muslims are required to pray five times a day. The first is at sunrise *Dhuha*, then there is *Dhuhr* (around noon), *Asr*, late afternoon, *Maghreb*, around sundown, and *Isha*, in the mid-evening. The *Fajr* prayer (around 4 am) is optional.

When I first came to Saudi Arabic I thought that the entire country stopped or closed down during prayers. I imagined traffic stopping in the street and drivers getting out of their cars to pray. This is not the case; traffic keeps moving. In the cities, cars may be seemingly abandoned haphazardly in front of mosques, but traffic will still move on the streets. In remote areas you may see drivers pull over onto the shoulder, get out of the car, put down a prayer rug in the direction of the *Qibla* and pray. Muslim employees will go to the prayer room or mosque and pray together. Employees must be given sufficient time to get to the mosque, pray and return to work. There are mosques in every neighborhood and they are a significant expense borne by the Saudi state budget. Sometimes the *muttawa* drive down the street in their black SUV's with bullhorns shouting gentle reminders to the Faithful.

During *salat*, telephones are often not answered unless the receptionist is a non-Muslim. All stores close for prayer. Customers will be asked to leave. In restaurants, the doors will close but diners will not be asked to leave their meals.

If you are visiting an office where the prayer room is not enclosed, please do not walk in front of the group praying. This is most disrespectful.

Except for the antics of the *muttawa* in malls, people are not forced to pray. Islam requires only that the religion be practiced to the best of one's ability. While there is a certain amount of peer pressure upon individuals to pray, even the Prophet Mohammad said that the relationship between man and God should not be interfered with by others.

There is a prayer room in the Al Khobar office but none in the office in Bahrain. Prayers are not ecumenical. You will not be invited to pray unless you have become a Muslim.

In Bahrain, the shi'a sect of Islam is officially recognized and practiced by a majority of the population. The shi'a pray only three times per day and tithe to their Imam, or religious leader. Shi'a mosque domes are tapered rather than round and sometimes display black flags in memory of Hussein, the Prophet's grandson who was killed at the battle of Karbala in 680 AD. I am told that there are shi'a mosques in Saudi Arabia but I have never seen one. Shi'ism is suppressed in Saudi Arabia–King Abdulazziz' troops, the *Ikhwan*, viewed the shi'a as polytheists deserving of death. In both the government and the private sector, shi'a are discriminated against in the Kingdom.

Crime and Punishment

Saudi Arabia has the reputation for being a strict country where punishments are imposed harshly. A person will lose his hand for theft and a repeat offender will lose another limb. Islam is the source of many of these punishments for crime but even pre-Islamic tribal punishments can be imposed when the circumstances warrant.

No trip to the Kingdom is complete without a visit to Chop Chop square, the place of public execution in Riyadh. This is the same place where the mail was dumped communally back in the days before privatization and is near the wooden door that was breached by King Abdulazziz in his successful effort to recover his family's Kingdom. A spearhead is still embedded in the door, and a guide will be happy to point it out. Of course, it may well be that this door has been replaced, restored, as it were, just like the restorations to the *QaâĂŹaba* overseen by the Custodian of the Two Holy Mosques. Executions take place on a Friday. Traditionally, executions were to take place at the mosque nearest to where the crime was committed, but Chop Chop square has become a popular place for Friday beheadings.

The standard form of execution in the Kingdom is beheading, though a woman who commits adultery will be stoned to death. This is actually a pre-Islamic punishment and is rarely applied. The method of its imposition is not the collection of a rabble to throw rocks; instead modern technology is preferred. The criminal is buried or made to sit while a dump truck full of rocks backs up—you can hear the beeping sound, an innovation imposed by U.S. plaintiff product liability lawyers on Detroit—it's safety first until the driver dumps the load of rocks on the victim. Women are otherwise entitled to equal treatment with men if they commit other crimes. A maid was beheaded in 2011 for murdering a child in her care.

The Saudis are not hypocrites about their exercise of capital punishment: in the United States executions take place out of site, behind closed doors, as if out of shame. Meanwhile, the Saudis proudly cut off heads in public. A few pre-Islamic punishments survive, such as crucifixion in the case of highway robbery. These are imposed at the scene of the crime as a warning to others. Not too long ago, a group of thieves hijacked an automobile and murdered four people. The judge (*qadi* in Arabic) decided that the pre-Islamic punishment for highway robbery was warranted. The bodies of the thieves were left to rot on crosses near Jeddah as a warning to others who might be tempted to engage in similar activity. You will not see any bodies decorating Chop Chop Square. After all, the stench could keep people away and so interfere with mail delivery.

I wonder what crucified bodies hanging by the side of the road does for tourism.

Even though the penalties can be terribly harsh they are not always imposed. It is said that only unrepentant recidivists face the harshest Islamic punishments but this fact is not widely disseminated to keep the population fearful and law-abiding. Losing a hand for theft is most often the penalty imposed for thieves who prey on pilgrims coming to the Great Mosque at Mecca. Otherwise, the goal of the Saudi prison system is rehabilitation. One of the ways that you can show that you are rehabilitated is by memorizing the Qu'ran. Memorize the entire book–some 40,000 words–and you may have the entirety of your sentence remitted. Memorizing only part of the text means a lesser sentence reduction.

It is said that Saudi Arabia has never executed a Westerner

for his crimes. Do not be the first.

Ramadan

The Holy Month of Ramadan is the ninth month of the Islamic, or hejira calendar. Because the Islamic calendar is a lunar calendar and shorter than the Gregorian calendar, hejira dates advance eleven days each year in comparison to the Gregorian calendar. What this means is that Ramadan can occur during any season or at any time during the year.

Observant Muslims fast during Ramadan. The fast must be kept from dawn to dusk only so that is why you can tuck into a 4:00 am early morning treat of grilled lamb before the sun rises with no guilt. Perhaps it is for this reason that most Saudis who keep the fast gain weight during the Holy Month. Because you are forbidden to eat during the day, you quickly find that all you can think about is food. It is human nature to excessively desire the forbidden. Fasting is thus as much psychological as it is physical. Because of the difficulty of getting on with normal life, many find Ramadan to be an excellent time for a vacation. If you are living in Riyadh, you will need to book your ticket well in advance.

Ramadan is also traditionally a time to give alms to the poor. The poor know this, of course, so expect them to show up unannounced at your office to give you an opportunity to meet your obligations. Some of these alms-giving and receiving relationships have endured over generations; and it is not uncommon for a alms-receiving father to introduce his sons to his funding sources. These alms-receivers will make but one annual visit during Ramadan to collect; so if you see strange people in the office do not assume that the firm is enlarging its client base.

Traditionally, the fast is broken by eating a few dates. The dates are followed, or accompanied by tea. After the tea comes a spread of lamb, chicken, beef, rice and other grilled meats, including goat.

Out of respect for your Muslim brothers and sisters, you are not permitted to eat or drink in their presence, whether in the office or out of doors. Not only is this considered culturally insensitive, it is an offense which could trigger police intervention. Closing the door to your office while you gorge yourself is an acceptable solution.

Office hours during Ramadan are changed to accommodate fasting Muslims. It is a universal practice in the Kingdom to have different working hours for Muslims and non-Muslims during Ramadan. For an office keeping traditional Saudi hours, the work hours for Muslims are from 10:00 am until 1:00 pm and then from 8:00 pm until 10:00 or 11:00 pm. For non-Muslims, the hours are from 9:00 to 5:00. For a Saudi office working a single shift, the schedule for Muslims is 10:00 am till 2:00 pm; and for non-Muslims, 9:00 am to 5:00 pm.

Business people have long ago come to grips with the realities of the situation and have despaired of accomplishing anything of importance during Ramadan. Every decision that needs to be made will be postponed. Meetings will be postponed. Ramadan is a good time to catch up with work or long term projects because your clients will assume that things are as slow in your office as they are in theirs and thus they will leave you alone.

What happens in Saudi Arabia during Ramadan is that day is traded for night. Expect traffic jams at 10:00 pm. Expect invitations to lunch at one in the morning. Schedules are simply reversed. While government offices are technically open, everyone who is fasting is feeling grumpy during the day. To a great extent, people just go through the motions during the day while waiting until it is time to leave.

Restaurants are closed during the day. Some close for the entire month; others will open for dinner only. In Bahrain the party is over until the end of the month. Even clandestine sources of supply will dry up until the month is over. In Bahrain, few places are permitted to serve alcohol and those few establishments permitted to sell alcohol will do so only in the evening. Nightclubs are shuttered. Some hotels will take a drink to your hotel room, but that is about it. The bars do not reopen until the Holy Month has passed. The only place where you can reliably get a drink in Ramadan during the day in Bahrain is at the British Club or the Rugby Club. During Ramadan only members are allowed inside the club during the day, so forget taking a client there. However, if you are not already a member you can arrange for a single month's membership for 15 BD or so.

Most shops are closed during the day as well. Grocery stores keep to an abbreviated schedule because after all, supplies for the fast-breaking meal have to be purchased somewhere. Live goats that have been slaughtered during the day are always available at Saudi butcher shops, but if a grocery store is closed the butcher shop will be closed too. You can see the skinned goats hanging in the shops' display windows. Mmmm.

In 1945 when King Abdulazziz met with Franklin Delano Roosevelt aboard the USS Quincy, the sailors did not know what to do with the live goats the Saudi king had brought onboard for his culinary needs. Apparently he did not yet trust American cuisine. If you share King Abdulazziz's passion for freshly-slaughtered goat you will have no difficulty fulfilling your dietary needs in the Kingdom. The eyeballs are considered a delicacy and it is a rare honor to be offered one by your host. The U.S. Military in their inimitable inventive way calls such a meal a "goat grab." Thankfully, goat is available during Ramadan as well as at all other times during the year.

Ramadan ends with the festival of *Eid al-adha*. For five days, government and private offices are closed. Then everyone comes back to work and complains that they are so far behind because no one was working during the past month. Unreasonable deadlines are imposed to encourage workers to catch up. The first two weeks after Ramadan are extremely busy as the Kingdom tries to regain lost ground.

Finally, the end of Ramadan is also an excellent time to go on a diet to lose all of the weight that you put on during a month of continuous fasting.

Supernatural

The supernatural cannot easily be ignored in Saudi Arabia. Despite the fact that you consider yourself a modern Westerner, and despite the fact that your Saudi colleagues have been schooled in the West, do not for a second think that the supernatural can be ignored or relegated to merely a minor role.

These same colleagues will be horrified if you tempt the evil eye and will blame the misfortune that has befallen you on your cavalier attitude towards such things. If you were to convert to and accept Islam, you would have less to worry about.

Muslims believe that there are beings called *djinn* which surround us. These are not ghosts; nor are they angels; they are not the spirits of the dead nor semi-divine beings but simply exist as another feature of God's creation. There are good *djinn* and bad *djinn*, there are Muslim *djinn* and *djinn* who have not yet heard God's message.

Do not be surprised if the Devil takes a particular interest in your affairs. This is only to be expected in a culture in which his presence must be avoided at all costs.

Witchcraft

Witchcraft in Saudi Arabia is no laughing matter. Though the Saudi authorities have recognized that shopping malls play a role in civil society beyond the mere acquisition of goods, they are also places where, supposedly, witchcraft is actively practiced.

A Saudi man noticed that his daughter was "acting strangely" when she was near a Sri Lankan maid at a shopping mall in Jeddah. When the child was moved away from the maid, the strange acts diminished. The logical conclusion—keep your child away from an unsavory-looking character—was not reached. Instead, the Saudi dad concluded that his daughter was being adversely affected by a spell cast by a witch. The possibility that a thirteen year old was acting up in the mall was outside his frame of reference. Instead, he immediately called the police, who upon investigation, reached the conclusion that witchcraft was indeed involved and arrested the witch.

All in the Year 2012.

Perhaps it is unfair to complain too much about witchcraft prosecutions in Saudi Arabia. In the U.K., suspected witches are simply murdered without judicial process. At least in Saudi Arabia you get all the due process you need before you are executed.

The difference is that in Saudi Arabia the police are arresting the suspected witches, while in the U.K., the police are receiving "training on helping children accused of witchcraft and sorcery." The Metropolitan Police even have a Religious Violence Unit whose chief officer noted that officers are currently not equipped to spot the danger signs pointing to accusations of witchraft and sorcery. In 2012, Eric Bikubi and Magalle Bamu were convicted of murdering Kristy Bamu, who was believed to be a witch bringing bad luck to the Bamu family. In the past ten years, according to *The Independent*, there have been 81 Metropolitan Police witchcraft investigations and 57 prosecutions.

Perhaps it is of little import that the Saudi and British police are on other sides of the issue as in both countries witchcraft cases end up in court nevertheless. The difference is that in Britain the killings are an extrajudicial crime while in Saudi Arabia the killings have the full force and majesty of the law behind them.

Since the supernatural deals with matters concerning the dead as well as the living, it is appropriate to mention burial practices in the Kingdom. It is a traditional Western custom to bury the dead six feet below the ground. Some say the practice grew up to protect bodies from grave robbers but the real reason is lost in time. In Saudi Arabia, the dead do not have their own gravestones, in fact, there are no gravestones at all. This is because the Wahabbi version of Saudi Islam abhors the veneration of the dead and does not want to admit the possibility of Muslim saints. After all, the basic tenet of Islam is that God has no partner.

All the dead then, from the King to the poorest visa overstayer, are wrapped in white cloth and taken to the cemetery, where the bodies are buried in a shallow pit eighteen inches below the surface. After six months, the dirt covering the body is removed, the body exposed to the elements, and then the dirt is put back. This process is repeated to speed decomposition until there is very little of the body left. Because of the decomposition, the unearthing of bodies, the continual biological processes, a Muslim cemetery has a very definite smell of death unlike landscaped Western cemeteries. The profession of grave tender is passed down from father to son.

In Riyadh, the only place where you will see dogs is at the cemetery. In Muslim countries they are considered to be unclean animals.

While shopping for scented candles at the mall it is unlikely that you will be mistaken for a witch but you never know. It is best to be prudent and to exercise caution.

Navy Base

There is a U.S. Navy Base in Bahrain (actually, "U.S. Navy Support Activity–Bahrain) which is the home of the U.S. Fifth Fleet and provides logistics services for U.S. Navy vessels in the region. There is a persistent belief that U.S. citizens can enter the base because they are U.S. citizens. This is not true. Unless you have military status of some kind—or know someone who does—you will not be allowed on the base. If you happen to have a CAC (Common Access Card) card, you can enter the base without any problem.

So what are you missing?

The base has ATM's that dispense U.S. dollars. You can use the U.S. Mail (for letters) at domestic rates. If you were in the military you would be able to receive mail as well, but this is a bit more complicated. So do not expect to be able to start your post-Ramadan diet with Jenny Craig diet meals as if you were in North America.

There is a liquor store that sells completely untaxed booze. The prices are cheaper than U.S. prices and much cheaper compared to prices in Bahrain. However, the store is relatively small so there is not a great deal of variety. If you arrive after an aircraft carrier has dropped anchor you will find that the selection has suffered greatly.

There is a Post Exchange which sells clothing, watches, electronics, and gifts. There is no commissary, but a well-stocked drug store (along the lines of a Walgreen's or Boots) has food items, pharmaceuticals and other supplies. Items that are prohibited in Bahrain and Saudi, such as the demonic Pepto-Bismol, can be found here.

There is a tailor shop, a barber shop and Western Union facilities to transfer money. There is an Internet cafe and all kinds of recreational facilities–a gym, racketball courts, tennis courts, movie theater, swimming pool, pool tables and more. There is a cafeteria offering inexpensive meals and "regular" coffee. There is also a food court where cherished American institutions such as Popeye's Chicken can be found. There are also educational facilities; two American universities have set up shop on the base. I do not know if you can register for courses without a CAC card but I think probably not.

To open up a Navy Federal Credit Union account on the base you will need a valid CAC card. Keep in mind that having a bank account on the base is not going to do you much good if you can't get past the guards in front.

There is a street called American Alley in the Juffair area where the base is located full of fast food restaurants—but no PopeyeâĂŹs—and T-shirt shops are strangely absent. On the Alley and in the neighborhood you will see many young (and not so young) military-types, most of whom have backpacks. A question provoking much speculation amongst expats concerns the contents of those backpacks and why they are being carried. Let me solve the mystery: the backpacks contain military uniforms. Under the Status of Forces Agreement with Bahrain, U.S. Military members are not permitted to wear their uniforms off-base. On-base, almost everyone is wearing a uniform. If you live off base, you carry your uniform with you and change after entry onto the base.

When you leave the base you will find an electronic sign reminding service members which places are off-limits to soldiers and sailors and warning of possible areas of civil disturbances. Other signs remind them to respect the laws, customs and traditions of Bahrain and not to dress immodestly. It is always interesting to find that a restaurant, hotel or other favorite Bahraini establishment has been condemned by U.S. military commanders.

Currently, the only way to get access to all of these wonderful facilities subsidized by the American taxpayer is to meet someone who works on the base who will agree to sponsor your entry. Perhaps you can have lunch at Popeye's.

Weekend Travel

There is a disconnect between the expectations of the new arrival and the reality encountered. People who come to Saudi Arabia are travelers, they are adventurous: they want to try new things. They come to Saudi Arabia thinking they will have two day weekends which, by switching with their colleagues or advantaging a three day weekend they can turn into four or five. The vision of regional vacations, of Europe and the 'stans fills their heads.

These visions are usually erased within the first month of arrival. Saudi Arabia has not signed an Open Skies aviation agreement. Flights into and out of the Kingdom are not routine, but events. The major carriers often have only one flight each day out of the Kingdom and these fill up fast. Not being able to get a reservation or a flight to or from the Kingdom is a real problem.

Interestingly enough, in many ways distances are mostly psychological. Flight time between Riyadh and Paris is roughly six hours, which is roughly the same distance as between New York and Los Angeles. Many people living in one city spend the weekend in the other and live bicoastal lives. The idea of spending the weekend (as short as it is) in London or Paris from Riyadh is pretty much inconceivable. A long weekend, perhaps.

Perhaps you will have a chance once in a blue moon.

Domestic flights are just as problematic. Business may demand that you be in Jeddah tomorrow (or your boss may promise your presence) but your travel agent may announce with the news that it will be at least a week before you can leave. Exiting the country must be planned and cannot be accomplished on a whim. Holidays are few and three day weekends rare. Up until 2002 it was necessary to obtain the permission of your sponsor to travel to the Eastern Province from Riyadh. Business trips are mostly inbound. The eager traveler will find that being stationed in Saudi Arabia is a disappointment.

This disappointment is one of the early crises that the candidate must survive. For a person used to traveling—after all, you have just come to Saudi Arabia—the feeling of being trapped can become overwhelming. Sitting in Riyadh and finding there are no flights out and there is not enough time to go to Bahrain and get back can be more than stifling.

Some seek solace in food or in a bottle. But most get over it and spend time on travel web sites planning trips that they will never take.

Do not come if you are planning on doing a lot of traveling. You won't be able to.

Weekends in Israel

Some people look at the map and think, well, if Saudi Arabia is so bad, perhaps I could spend time in a country that is a little more accommodating and Western. I have heard more than one person express a desire to spend weekends in Israel because it is so close. After winning a Saudi government contract, one major

Western consulting company flew its personnel in and out of the Kingdom from Beirut every week. The program ended when the Israelis bombed the runway at the Beirut airport. Saudi Aramco flies its people from remote locations back and forth every week to the paradise that is Dhahran.

A weekend trip to Israel is only theoretically possible. There are no flights from Saudi Arabia to Israel. The easiest way to get there is via Amman, Jordan, but there will is a twelve-hour layover. You could go by car and cross into the West Bank by land. Returning would be by the same method. Another possibility is to fly to Cyprus. Cyprus Air has flights several times per week from Riyadh to Lanarca and from Lanarca you could fly to Tel Aviv. Or you could go by boat. It is possible to travel by sea from Cyprus to Israel, it is just not practical for a weekend trip which commenced in Saudi Arabia.

If after these warnings you want to make the trip anyway, go right ahead. The Israelis will not stamp your passport. The received wisdom is that if you have traveled to Israel you will not be permitted to travel to Saudi Arabia. This is not true, though if your passport is full of Israeli stamps (perhaps from all of your weekend trips there) you may have difficulties at the border, but no worse than, say, an American citizen who is not ethnically Cuban trying to explain his visits to the beaches at Varadero to a dubious immigration officer.

In truth, spending weekends in Israel, Lebanon, Jordan or Damascus (get your visa in advance) is not possible not so much because of distance but lack of available air transportation and the shortened Saudi weekend.

If you must get out, the options are the Saudi desert, Bahrain, the Emirates or Oman. That is about it.

Day Trips from Riyadh

Another possibility for weekend travel is to stay in the Kingdom and explore. In the desert, life is full of mysteries and moves at a different pace. A group of Riyadhis decided one weekend to go into the desert. They traveled in four-wheel drive vehicles equipped with GPS systems, brought extra water and gasoline, ice, food, satellite phones, tents, radios, flares and all other manner and type of emergency equipment, just in case. Arriving in the deep desert, they set up camp, only to be passed, after about an hour, by a friendly bedouin who was walking around with no equipment whatsoever as if taking a stroll down Fifth Avenue. Of course, they had him in for tea.

Slavery

Slavery was practiced legally in Saudi Arabia until 1967. Many of those still alive can remember the institution. Some of those who owned slaves are alive as well as those born into slavery. The remnants of slavery are seen even today. Slavery, recognized in both the Bible and the QuâĂŹran, has long been practiced in the Arabian Peninsula. As late as 2003, a slave market was said to still operate in Jeddah. It was once common for the wealthy to purchase a playmate for their children. The slave child without a last name grew up alongside his owner's child. Some of these relationships outlasted slavery and persist even today.

Even though slavery has officially been abolished its customs and practices persist even in the vocabulary of voluntary employment. The vocabulary of slavery is in common parlance An employee does not resign, he "absconds." People do not leave the service of their employer, they become "runaways." This shameful vocabulary is still seen on a daily basis in the Kingdom. You will read in the Arab News stories about how a maid "absconded," though in North America the term would be "resigned" and the event would hardly be news. The "maid crisis" the country is suffering in 2011 is a direct result of the Government of Indonesia prohibiting domestic workers from being sent to Saudi Arabia because of poor treatment. This was triggered by the beheading of an Indonesian maid in 2011. She had been sentenced to death after murdering her employer after suffering abuse. Even though a Saudi ambassador officially apologized, the Government of Indonesia has so far refused to change course without the implementation of reforms.

The incidents of indentured servitude are well-established in the law. You will find that there are many things you cannot accomplish in the country without the consent of your sponsor, who must even give his consent for you to change jobs or return to the country after resigning.

One way of dealing with the guilt you might have working in and around such a system is by becoming an employer yourself. You will have no difficulty employing a maid or a houseboy for approximately 1000 SAR per month, which is less than $300. If you decide to do so; try to make their lives better and increase their salaries.

Lies

One of the most disconcerting phenomena you will encounter in your day to day business dealings is the prevalence of aspirational thinking. Simply put, aspirational thinking is stating as fact something that you wished were true. It is not always immediately apparent that you are dealing with a departure from reality. Some Westerners react with revulsion to the practice, which they call "lying." It is not, though unfortunately, the seasoned practitioner of aspirational thinking will make pronouncements that are often indistinguishable from flat-out falsehoods.

Imagine if someone said to you, "I own a red automobile." You would expect that the speaker indeed owned a red automobile. However, in Saudi Arabia if you were to ask to see the vehicle, you would quickly find that no such vehicle exists. Imagine if the phrase, "I wish I owned..." was placed immediately before the statement of ownership. Or, "wouldn't it be nice if I owned" or even, "Once upon a time, I owned" or variations of the above preceded the assertion.

In the Kingdom, this aspirational qualifier is understood. It takes a very long time to become conversant with Saudi culture to the point where you can understood that the qualifier is missing and that when someone tells you that he has every single Saudi law on his computer he is only expressing a wish in the same way that a child might write a letter to Santa Claus asking for a fire truck. The aspirational phrase is always used to describe wealth or travel. As a new consultant working in Saudi Arabia, you will often fail to recognize the implied aspirational phrase and so reach the erroneous conclusion that you are constantly being lied to. Your boss will tell you that you need to meet with him the next morning for an important meeting. That night, he will leave for Europe without telling you. You will be enraged. Do not be. This is just a stage you will pass through in the process of acculturation. Soon you will believe no one. You will even begin to lie to your own friends and family about the most insignificant of matters with great fluency.

The writ of the Ten Commandments does not run to the Arabian Peninsula. Lying, per se, is not necessarily a sin in Islam. After the Battle of Badr, the Prophet Mohammad advised that it is appropriate to lie if doing so would help the cause of the Muslims. Since Muslims are commanded to imitate their prophet, this means that there is religious approval for lying if it is your best interests to do so.

It is bad form to confront someone with his own aspirational statement. If you have the temerity to do so, do not expect that the liar (*kathab* in Arabic) will admit to his fault because for him it is not a fault at all. The usual response in such a situation is yet another lie. If you confront that lie, you will merely get another, and so on. This is a fool's game so there is no reason to play. Simply respect the rhythm and rituals of the country and lie yourself. After a while, it will be second nature and any ideas that you might have had about lying will be forgotten due to your new skill at deception.

Banking

In Saudi Arabia cash is king. While credit and debit cards are widely used, checks are not. Saudi Arabia is the only country where you might find cash counting machines on both sides of the teller window. I do not know if this is to keep the tellers honest or is simply a courtesy because it would take too long to verify the count manually. Checks in the Kingdom are viewed with suspicion. Even cashier's or certified checks have become fraud vehicles and are distrusted.

An experienced Saudi teller is nothing less than a magician. I have seen Saudi tellers open the wrapping of a brick of $100 bills fresh from the U.S. Federal Reserve and pick out the correct number of bills from the brick just by feel. The riffling cash counting machine only confirms what the teller already knows. Bricks contain ten $10,000 packs of $100 dollar bills. Their 22-pound specialty Crane paper has not touched human hands since being shrink-wrapped after passing through the intaglio presses of the government. But if you already know this you probably don't need this orientation guide. Or a job, for that matter.

Exchanging money at the King Khalid International Airport in Riyadh is never a problem. The currency exchange facilities are open on a 24 hour basis (I have not checked on Fridays, the only time when 24 hours per day is more like 18). You do not have to show a passport or a plane ticket and there is no need to go through security. In the armored room with a teller window there are usually enough bricks to service all travelers. Change your money before you leave the airport. You will get the best rates and changing funds in the city can be an ordeal. Facilities in Dammam, Jeddah and Bahrain are also available on a 24 hour basis.

While you can exchange more than SR 60,000, if you try to take this much cash out of the country you will have to file a customs currency declaration. It is not illegal to take any amount of currency out of the country, but failure to file the declaration is a violation. It is also required to declare jewelry or gold that you may be carrying.

While there are numerous signs advising travelers of the requirement, I have never heard of this law being enforced. Asking for the form will only create all sorts of chaos. The law was issued to assuage the Americans; the Kingdom had never had a problem in this area before. To a great extent then, this law, like several others in the Kingdom, is cosmetic.

Automatic teller machines are found throughout Saudi Arabia and are connected to the major international cash networks. You will have no difficulty pulling cash from your account while in Saudi Arabia.

If you need money wired to you–or you wish to wire money yourself–there are Western Union outlets in both Saudi Arabia and Bahrain. In Saudi Arabia you can also use the facilities of the Al Rajhi Bank–they will be happy to wire money for you as long as you can identify yourself. They will give you an identification card which will make it easier for you to wire money in the future. This identification number is not strictly speaking an account since you cannot make deposits.

You can pay your American Express bill locally at the Saudi American bank or American Express outlets.

The *halawa* system also exists in Saudi Arabia. If you need to send money in the region it is less expensive than Western Union. The system has come under suspicion since 9/11 because of accusations that the network has been used for terrorist financing. If you need to send funds to remote regions sometimes it is the only realistic choice.

When you move to a new location it is often recommended that you obtain a local bank account to facilitate local business. But in Saudi Arabia it is best to resist the temptation to open a local account for several reasons.

You will not be able to open an account unless you have an *iqama*. So if getting an *iqama* is not in your future there is nothing to be worried about. The problem with the requirement is that in the Kingdom foreigners' bank accounts are linked to their immigration status. This means that if you go out of status–or worse, you are reported as having gone out of status even if you have not–your bank account will be frozen and your access to your money will be blocked.

Sorting matters out is no easy task because three separate institutions are involved. Each will point the finger at the other while hinting that you are the one to blame. These institutions are not set up to troubleshoot cooperatively. The Passport Office tells the bank based on information received from your employer to freeze your account. Your bank will say that they are only following orders from the Passport Office and they have no discretion in the matter. The Passport Office—if fortune smiles at you and you can find the appropriate official—will claim that he is merely acting upon information supplied by your employer.

Meanwhile, your employer will claim that he has done nothing to initiate the process. Calling a lawyer and asking for assistance will only complicate matters and spawn a school of conflicting narratives. Because you are a consultant you think you should be able to handle such a problem. But you will not be able to. Perhaps a colleague will claim that he has *wasta* (influence) and can solve your problem, but this is aspirational thinking and in fact he cannot help.

Foreign embassies often have to get involved in these cases because there is no other real alternative. No one wants the embarrassment of leaving a family destitute. Leaving the country is often no solution because there are no funds for an exit permit and your employer is concerned that you will leave and never come back.

If you are desperate, one technique is to pack your suitcase and go to the police station. Stand around outside the facility with a hang-dog look on your face. Eventually a policeman will approach. He will take you to an English-speaking officer. You can then explain that you have overstayed your visa and ask to be deported. Your request will usually be accommodated.

This last-resort practice has grown up because employers often simply stop paying their employees because they have run out of funds to do so. Living paycheck to paycheck, the employees have no money to pay for a plane ticket home and they cannot work for a solvent employer because their *iqama* is linked to their bankrupt employer.

To further complicate matters, the Saudi authorities have announced that they will start monitoring employee (i.e. *iqama-holder*) bank accounts to make sure that there are no deposits not accounted for given the employee's salary as stated in his employment contract. This can only create bureaucratic mischief.

Under the new system, if you sell the living room couch and deposit the proceeds in your account in the middle of the month, red flags will go off and your account may be frozen. After all, there is no easy way to tell if you are merely the vendor of a used couch or a drug or alcohol kingpin. It is not clear if SAMA, the Saudi Arabian Monetary Agency, is going to monitor the accounts; at present it is not clear which agency will do so. Adding yet another institution to the mix is nothing less than a guarantee of more commotion, more trouble and more improperly-frozen accounts. There is a another perfect word in Arabic to describe such a situation: *fitna*, which is loosely translated as chaos.

To be safe, avoid getting a local bank account. Your money is probably safer under the mattress, especially if you have failed to tape the toilets and the mattress is guarded by a rat.

Banking in Saudi Arabia ranges from the rabble queuing at a Western Union to the private banking facilities of the Al Rajhi Bank, the favorite bank of the Saudi royal family. At the bank you will find a comfortable chair in front of the teller window if you need to need to sully yourself by getting close to a teller at all. Otherwise you can drink tea in the bank manager's office while bank personnel caters to all your needs. No request involving finances is considered impossible, unusual or incapable of compliance.

In one case a Saudi prince had a dispute with a commoner. The commoner had somehow obtained a judgment against him and levied on the prince's account at the Al Rajhi bank. Given the Saudi judicial system, this was no small feat. The Saudi prince did not appreciate the hard work that had gone into obtaining the order of garnishment. The bank manager told the prince that the garnishment was in good order and that compliance with court orders is not optional in Saudi Arabia. The prince, accompanied by an entourage of rifle-carrying Bedouins, did not agree. The prince advised the bank manager that the funds would be returned to his account immediately, or else.

The police responded quickly to a report of rifle-bearing men entering the Royal bank. When they arrived, they quickly determined who was involved and apologized to the bank manager that the matter was out of their hands. The bank manager quickly concluded that his previous compliance was in error after all and that the funds would be restored immediately to the prince's account.

Try getting service like that at Coutts.

Saudiization

"Saudiization" is a term you will hear from time to time during your stay in the Kingdom. There is a dire need to provide employment opportunities for Saudi nationals. Part of the problem is that while office jobs are highly prized, Saudis will not accept jobs which they consider demeaning, such as a position which includes any kind of manual labor.

Initially, businesses were told that at least 30% of their workforce should be Saudi. Some sectors of the economy are fully Saudiized, such as the banking sector, while the task of nationalizing other sectors has been less successful. Several years ago there was a requirement to restrict taxicab companies from hiring foreign drivers. There was an outcry—even though the taxicab companies are all Saudi-owned—because of high costs. After a while, the requirement was quietly abandoned. In 2012 the Government announced that it will try again.

The latest effort is the new *nitaqat* (in Arabic, "limits") system. Under this system, companies are assigned color codes based on the number of Saudi employees working for them. A company classified "green" is in full compliance, "yellow" nearly compliant and "red" non-compliant. Non-Saudi employees working for a red company may change their employment to a new employer without the need of obtaining the old employer's consent. Note that even under this new program the vestiges of indentured servitude remain present. It is unclear whether the new system will be any more successful than the old one. One can expect that Saudi employers will continue to resist hiring their own nationals and that foreign companies will follow their example.

Miscellaneous

Capital Club

The Capital Club is a business club founded by one of the members of Bahrain's royal family. It is on the 52nd floor of the middle building in the Gulf Financial Harbour, the same building which houses a mostly closed shopping mall and a five minute walk from the Yorks Bahrain office. The club has an extraordinary view of the sea as well as the city of Manama and is a pleasant place to take clients.

While Yorks has a corporate membership, only partners may join. Even where associates offer to pay to join, the offer will be rejected. You will be graciously invited from time to time to the Club and there is no reason not to accept the invitation. Otherwise, as far as Yorks is concerned, the Capital Club is not for you. Being excluded from a club only heightens the desire to belong. It is for that reason that velvet ropes stand outside often-empty night clubs, not to control capacity but so that those who enter will feel privileged. From time to time you will wish that you had your very own membership.

Fortunately, there is a solution. The Capital Club is a full member of Signature Clubs International, so joining one club that is a member of the network will give you access to all sister clubs. The Petroleum Club of Houston has an especially sympathetic view of our situation in the Gulf and has provided facilities to solve the membership issue. You can contact the Petroleum Club in Houston to obtain your non-resident membership for a fraction of the normal initiation fee, and for about the same amount of money you would have spent had Yorks accepted your offer to pay for membership in the first place.

Cinemas

There are no movie theaters in Saudi Arabia. It is thought immoral for unrelated men and women to be sitting together in the dark. Given that there is a doctrine of Islamic family law jurisprudence covering "fornication by mistake" this cannot be too much of a surprise. When extended families slept together in tents there was a risk of rolling left instead of rolling right. Theaters in Saudi Arabia present a similar moral hazard.

The closest theaters are in Bahrain, where one can find lightly censored-films watched by audiences of avid Saudis who have traveled to the little Kingdom for the experience.

From an architectural point of view, there are several theater-like venues in the Kingdom. These are used mostly for conferences. Somehow dimming the lights for a Powerpoint presentation is less sinful than for a film. Given that women attending these conferences are separated from the men and seated in their own "Women's Section" there is not much of a risk of immoral behavior. Films have been shown at such conferences; there are facilities at at the Prince Mohammad bin Fahd University in the Eastern Province where the promotional film *Arabia* premiered in November, 2011. There were several dignitaries at the event, some of them women, who were allowed to watch the film from the comfort and security of the women's section.

Entertainment

There is an edition of the British travel magazine *Time Out* for Bahrain. There is no similar guide for the Eastern Province. Or Riyadh. Or anywhere else in the Kingdom of Saudi Arabia for that matter.

Begging

Begging in Saudi Arabia is an honorable profession, with its own code, regulations, customs, traditions and practices. It is common to see beggars in Saudi Arabia carrying documents, which they happily show you—or shove in your face. Any request for money needs to have the proper paperwork. The document, usually from a charitable hospital, should bear the seal of the Chamber of Commerce a facsimile thereof, or at least a passable forgery. The alms-seeker's medical condition should be in writing, in a font size which is easy to read at a speed of approximately 2.0 kilometers per hour at a distance of one meter, because the document may also be shown to drivers when their automobiles come to a stop at a traffic light. Without proper documentation, the chances of a donation are lessened.

The Beggar's Code of Ethics is scrupulously followed, but disputes between the supplicants sometimes end in violence. In a recent case, a beggar normally stood outside a mosque asking for alms. He proudly possessed a certificate of ill-health, describing a tumor that he had been dying from for the past ten years. One day, he took the certificate into the mosque in make a more direct appeal for funds from the worshipers. After making his presentation, he returned to his strategic spot outside the mosque's door, only to find that a colleague with a crutch had occupied his position. The two argued; the crutch became a weapon. The worshipers tried to break up the fight between the two surprisingly vigorous men but in the end the police had to be called.

Shopping

There is an excellent chain of office supplies stores in Saudi Arabia called the Jarir Bookstore. You will be able to find most of what you need there. Jarir also carries books in English, newspapers, mobile telephones, laptop computers, art supplies in addition to general office equipment. Outside the bookstore, you will often find vendors selling nuts like cashews and pistachios in bulk as well as chewing sticks known as *mishwak*. The sticks are an old desert-style implement for cleaning the teeth when water is at a premium. Letter-size paper is not used in the Kingdom, the standard A4 size is used instead. If you need letter-size paper you can sometimes find it at Jarir or one of the grocery stores on the Aramco compound —if you can get in.

There are a few office supply stores on Exhibition Road in Bahrain, near the *Crawn Plaza* hotel, which of course, has nothing to do with the Crowne Plaza. There is another small store in the suq which does a decent job. Otherwise, office supplies can be obtained at Geant or Lulu hypermarkets. The Bahrain bookstore chain, called Jashanmal, does not carry office supplies but depending on the location, may carry upscale items such as expensive pens, perfume, dishware and luggage. By the way, in Saudi Arabia Geant was sold to Panda. The other French hypermarket chain, Carrefour, is found in both countries.

The other large supermarket chain in the Kingdom is Tamimi Supermarkets. They have been around much longer than the others. They sell U.S. Safeway branded products and are found throughout the Kingdom. They claim to be open 24 hours a day but you will find them closed on Fridays until after prayers.

On Friday mornings, stores and gas stations are closed. It will be difficult to find anything open. You may have some luck at the airport, but that is about it. The gas station in front of the old airport in Riyadh is sometimes open. In Bahrain many stores, restaurants and markets are open on Fridays. People complain about the increase in prices for food in Saudi Arabia but except for exotic items you will find that the prices are comparable or lower than those in North America.

Fast Food

Some people are surprised to find that all (or nearly all) of their favorite fast food restaurants are present in Saudi Arabia and Bahrain. This really should be no surprise. There is a KFC in Fallujah, Iraq. During the Iraq war a mob killed and strung up the burnt bodies of a group of American defense contractors, but the restaurant was not touched. The demonstrators were not about to let their political views interfere with access to the Colonel's special blend of herbs and spices.

There are a few nods to local tastes. In McDonald's you will find the McArabia sandwich, which you are unlikely to find outside the region. When you enter one of these fine dining establishments, you may be surprised to see trays carrying the remnants of meals on tables. The local practice is to leave your mess on the table. The staff will clean up after you. If due to habit you try to clean up after yourself you will only draw stares. The real difficulty is what happens when you get used to the practice and return home. There the stares will be because you have left your mess on the table and the staff has not been trained to clean up after you.

If you are hungry after working late at night you should know about *shawarma*. *Shawarma* (either beef or chicken) is a popular type of sandwich in the Kingdom. This is not a Saudi delicacy per se (it is called gyros in Greece and–not surprisingly–*shawarma* in Israel) but it is useful for those late nights working at the office. *Shawarma* is made during the day but is sold only in the evenings. So if you want a *shawarma* for lunch, you are pretty much out of luck.

The One Question

Whenever you leave the office and the Middle East on a business or personal trip, you will be asked one question within a day or so. The question is, "when are you coming back?" The reason why the question is asked is because it is assumed that you will not come back. This is in part due to Saudi insecurity, but there is more than one tale about a consultant who, leaving work, drove his car to the airport, parked in the lot in Riyadh—there is no long term or short-term lot, there is merely a single lot costing about SR 50 per day–and the next day called the office to tell the secretary where the car was and to ship his personal effects.

The terminal vacation is also popular—you go on vacation and you never return. Saudis know that their country is difficult to live in and they feel that at any moment you might abandon ship. Whether this affects all of your dealings with Saudis is hard to say.

The Work

This guide is an orientation manual for living in the Eastern Province and Bahrain. So discussing the work that you will be doing is what consultants would say, outside the scope. Sorry.

Basic Information

Official Name:
Kingdom of Saudi Arabia

Political System:
Monarchy

The King & Prime Minister:
King Abdullah Bin Abdul Aziz Al-Saud, Custodian of the Two Holy Mosques

System of Governance:
Basic Law of Governance which includes the following statutes:

Article 7:
Governance in the Kingdom of Saudi Arabia derives its authority from the Holy Quran and the *Sunnah* of Prophet Mohammed, both of which govern this law and all the laws of the state.

Article 8:

Governance in the Kingdom of Saudi Arabia shall be based on justice, shura (consultation), and equality, in accordance with the Islamic shari'a.

Location:

The Kingdom of Saudi Arabia lies at the furthermost part of southwestern Asia. It is bordered to the west by the Red Sea; to the east by the Arabian Gulf, Qatar and the United Arab Emirates; to the north by Kuwait, Iraq and Jordan; and to the south by Yemen and the Sultanate of Oman.

Capital:

Riyadh

Area:

2 million square kilometers

Climate:

Tropical climate, generally hot in summer (up to 50 C), cooler in winter.

Main Cities:

Riyadh, Jeddah, Dammam, Makkah, Madinah, Taif

Administrative Division of the Kingdom:

The Kingdom of Saudi Arabia is composed of 13 administrative regions, each comprising a number of provinces. The Kingdom includes 43 provinces of category (A) and 61 provinces of category (B).

Official Language:

Arabic, although English is commonly used, especially in commercial correspondence

Business Hours:

Government Offices:

7:30 to 14:30

Banks:

9:30 to 16:30 (Saturday to Wednesday)

Private Sector:

Varies from one business to another and from place to place. During Ramadan, most enterprises open in the evening.

Official Holidays:

Weekend:

Thursday and Friday

Eid al-Fitr:

From 25th Ramadan to 5th Shawwal

Eid al-Adha:

From 5th Dhul Hajja to 15th Dhul Hajja

National Day:

September 23

All government institutions and departments are closed during these holidays. In the private sector, it differs from business to business.

Standard Time:

GMT + 3 hours Saudi Arabia does not follow Summer or Daylight Savings Time; during these periods the Kingdom is two hours ahead of London.

Currency:

The Saudi Riyal (SR) which is divided into 100 Halalas

US$ Exchange Rate:

1USD = SR 3.75

Unit of Measure/Weight:

Metric system/kilogram

Electricity Voltage:

Both 110V and 220V

Country/Dialing Codes:

+966 for the country code plus the city code as follows:
    Riyadh (1)
    Jeddah (2)
    Dammam (3);
    mobiles (55) or (56)

Internet Code:

.sa

Cost of Public Utilities:

Electricity

1. Industry:

All consumption categories $ 0.033/kilowatt-hour (KWH) of monthly consumption

2. Agriculture:

Price varies from $0.013ÃŘ$0.032/KWH of monthly consumption, based on consumption categories

3. Commercial/residential:

Price varies from $0.013-$0.070/KWH of monthly consumption, based on consumption categories

Water:

Price for a cubic metre (m3) ranges from $0.03-$1.60, based on consumption categories

Fuel:

Gasoline (95): $0.20/liter
 Gasoline (91): $0.16/liter
 Kerosene: $0.17/liter
 Diesel: $0.10/liter
 Gas: $0.75/million units

Population (2008)

Total Population:

24.8 million

Population Growth Rate:

2.3%

Population Distribution by Sex:

Male: 55.2% Female: 44.8%

Population Distribution by Nationality:

Saudis: 73% Non-Saudis: 27%

Population Distribution by Age:

Below 15: 32.3%
15-39: 45.9%
40+: 21.8%

Dependency Ratio:

54%

Population Distribution by Region:

Riyadh: 24.5%
Makkah: 25.1%
Eastern Province: 14.7%
Asir: 7.3%
Madinah: 6.8%
Other regions: 21.6%

Labor Market

Total Labor Force:

8.45 million
Saudis: 49.4%
Non-Saudis: 50.4%

Total Labor Force in Government Sector:

1.18 million
   Saudi: 92%
   Non-Saudis: 8%

Total Labor Force in Private Sector:

6.84 million
   Saudis: 40.1%
   Non-Saudis: 59.9%

Employment Distribution by Sector:

Construction and Building: 12.8%
   Wholesale and Retail Trade: 19.4%
   Community, Social, and Personal: 31.2%
   Manufacturing Industries: 6.6%
   Agriculture, Forests, and Fishing: 3.8%
   Other Sectors: 26.2%

Labor Costs:

The average cost for labor in the private sector (Males) is $358/month. The average cost for labor in the private sector (Females) is $483/month.

Useful Links

Ministry of Agriculture www.agrwat.gov.sa
   Ministry of Economy & Planning www.planning.gov.sa
   Ministry of Foreign Affairs www.mofa.gov.sa

Ministry of Petroleum & Minerals www.mopm.gov.sa
Ministry of Labor www.mol.gov.sa
Ministry of Finance www.mof.gov.sa
Ministry of Commerce & Industry www.commerce.gov.sa
The Supreme Economic Council: www.sec.gov.sa
Shura Council: www.shura.gov.sa
Saudi Industrial Development Fund: www.sidf.gov.sa
Saudi Arabia General Investment Authority: www.sagia.gov.sa
The Supreme Commission for Tourism: www.sct.org.sa

Chambers of Commerce & Industry:

Council of Saudi www.saudichambers.org.sa
    Riyadh www.riyadhchamber.org.sa
    Jeddah Chamber of Commerce & Industry www.jcci.org.sa
    Eastern Province www.chamber.org.sa
    Medina Chamber of Commerce & Industry www.madcci.com
    Taif www.taifchamber.org.sa
    Makkah www.makcci.com
    Qassim www.qcc.org.sa
    Al-Majma'a www.majcci.org.sa
    Tabuk www.tcci.org.sa
    Al-Ahsa www.alhasachamber.com.sa
    Abha www.abhacci.org.sa
    Hail www.hail-chamber.com.sa
    Najran www.najranchamber.com.sa
    Al-Qurayat www.gurayat-cci.org.sa

Council of Saudi Chambers

P.O. Box 16683

Riyadh, Saudi Arabia 11474
Tel: 966-1-405-3200
Fax: 966-1-402-4747
Website: www.saudichambers.org.sa
Email: council@saudichambers.org.sa

Emergency Telephone Numbers

Civil Defense: 998
   Police: 999
   Traffic Police: 993
   Passports: 992
   Ambulance: 997

Index

Arabizi, 75
Djinns, 65, 105
Time Out Bahrain, 130
abaya, 20
iqama, 10
niqab, 20

Airlines, 14
    Code Shares, 15
    Dammam Airport, use of discouraged, 16
Alcohol, 91
    sid, 94
    AA, 95
    luggage, 16
    Package Stores, 94
    Whiskey
        Johnny Walker, 91, 93, 94
Arrival, 14
    Hotel, 22
Ataturk, Kemal, 77

Automobile Purchase, 10
Automobiles, 17, 18
    Driving, 30
        chaos, 30
        death cars, 31
        engine fires, 32
        vandalism, 33
        Women, 85
    Traffic Laws, 30

Bank Account, 10
Banking, 120
Bar on Re-entry, 9
Bedouin Raiders, 14
Bedouins, 125
Blue Flame(book), 91
British Bombers, 93
British Club, 6
Burial Practices, 107

Capital Club, 24, 128
Caravans, 14
Carrefour, 132

INDEX

Cash, 19
Cassock(*thobe*, 20
Cats, 53
Cemeteries, 108
Censhorship, 62
Censorship
    Airlines, 14
Chaos, 30, 121, 124
Cinemas, 129
Coptic Christians, 90
Coutts Bank, 125
Crash Helmet, 20
Customs Duties, 5

Day Trips, 115
Diversity, 89
Donuts, 26
Dress Code, 20
Driver's License, 5
Dylan, Bob, 87

Electricity
    Bahrain, 50
    Saudi Arabia, 48
Embassy
    Saudi Arabia, 8

Falsehood, 118
    Aspirational Qualifier, 118
Fees
    Bahrain, 11

Gasoline, 32
Gender, 83
Girl's School Fire, 81
Goat Grab, 104
Golf Carts, 44
Ground Transportation, 16
    Buses, 17
    Limo Service, 18
    Rental Cars, 17
    Taxis, 25, 26, 36, 126
        Drivers, kindred with, 17

Harassment of Women, 84
Hard Rock Café, 88
Hardship Post, 24
Hotel
    Bible, 23
    Khozama, 88
    Mövenpeck, 88
    Minibar, 23
    Royal Meridian, 88
Housing, 42–47
    Aramco Compound, 43
    Aramco Contractors, 45
    Employee
        Bahrain, 46
        KSA, 45
    Rental Terms, 46

IKEA, 58, 85
Influence, 123

International Borders, 35–41
Ireland
    and Sudanese emigration, 42
Israel, 113

Jarir Bookstore, 131
Jashanmal, 131

Language, 74
Law Enforcement, 79

Mail, 60
Marriage, 86
    Temporary, 87
McDonald's, 39, 41, 71, 132
Medical Exam, 9

NASCAR, 31
National Guard, 79
Navy Base, 109

Panhandlers, 130
PeptoBismol, 61
Photographs, need for, 6
Postal Codes, 5
Pound,Ezra, 69
Prosperity Well, 44
Punishment, 98
    Beheading, 98
    Crucifixion, 99
    Stoning, 98

Raban,Jonathan, 39, 72
Rats, 54
Religion, 96
    Prayer Times, 96, 97
    Ramadan, 101–104
Religious Police, 80, 82, 88
Riyadh River, 51

Sandwich,Pork , 71
Satan, 61
Saudi Aramco
    Bulletin Board, 19
Saudiization, 126
Secret Police, 80
Security
    and bilingualism, 45
Shipping Personal Effects, 4
Skype, 64
Slavery, 116
Sponsorship, 12
Submarine, 24

Tamimi Supermarkets, 132
Television, 63
Terrorism, 65
Tijuana, 70
Toilets, need to tape, 54–59
Traffic Laws
    one-lane exit ramp, scarcity of, 30
Tribes, 77

Uncle Sam's, 92

INDEX

Visas, 7, 35
    iqama, 8, 63, 122, 123
    CPR, 11, 19
    Work Permit, 8

Water, 51
Weekend Travel, 112
Western Union, 121
Witchcraft, 81, 106, 107
Work Week, 27
    Weekend, 27

Yorks
    Address, 5
    Bahrain Office, 24
    Calgary, 2

Dreaming, 37
Dress Code, 29
Ghosts, 66
Khobar Office, 25
    public transportation, lack of, 26
moving heaven and earth, 22
Office Hour, 28
One office two locations, 24
Punishment, 22
Secret Switch, 28
Sudanese landlord, 43
Visas, 12
Yorks Services, 1

www.ingramcontent.com/pod-product-compliance
Lightning Source LLC
Chambersburg PA
CBHW072043290426
44110CB00014B/1559